Joyfully Serving Christ

What Is Critical?

Marjorie Tatter

Joyfully Serving Christ

What Is Critical?

Marjorie Tatter

Copyright © Marjorie Tatter 2017

All rights reserved. No part of this book may be used or reproduced by any means, graphic, electronic or mechanical, including photocopying, recording or taping or by any information storage retrieval system without the written permission of the publisher except in the case of brief quotations embodied in critical articles and reviews.

Whosoever Press books may be ordered through booksellers or by contacting:

Whosoever Press
10749 AL. Hwy 168
Boaz, AL 35957

www.whosoeverpress.com
1-256-706-3315

Because of the dynamic nature of the Internet, any web addresses or links contained in this book may have changed since publication and may no longer be valid. The views expressed in this work are solely those of the author and do not necessarily reflect the views of the publisher, and the publisher hereby disclaims any responsibility for them.

ISBN-13: 978-0-9987724-8-6 (sc)

ISBN-13: 978-1724586841

Library of Congress Control Number: Applied For

Printed in the United States of America
Whosoever Press date: 6/1/2018

Table of Contents

What is Critical? What is Often Overlooked?..................3

Who?..................12

What?..................27

When?..................110

Where?..................121

Why is it Important to Know the Proper Order and Names of the Book in the Bible?..................126

Why is it Important to Have a Separate Bible and Not Just Depend on Your IPAD?..................128

Pictures..................130

What is Critical? What is Often Overlooked?

Do you know about Raymond Raikes? He is credited with organizing and starting the first Sunday schools in the world near London, England in the mid 1760's. Because public schools were nonexistent and financial times were precarious, only the gentry or upper-class children had **the benefit of organized education.** The middle and lower-class children had to work hard in factories **six days a week. Whatever free time they found was occupied largely by thieving.** Raikes knew that these working children were just as capable of learning as **the wealthier.** He cared about these **precious, illiterate souls, and wanted them to forsake their lives of theft and godlessness upon learning of the love of Christ**, the Ten Commandments, and the Golden Rule. **And so, taking advantage of the first massed produced** Bibles, Raymond Raikes established Sunday Schools to teach children to read, using as their textbook, the **Holy** Bible.(All about the Sunday school-David J. Fant and Addie Marie French-second edition)

By the early 1800's Sunday schools had spread to the New World especially on the east coast of the United States. It should be noted that in the New England area, the congregational churches had catechism classes teaching the basic doctrines of their churches as early as 1669 but not necessarily on Sunday with children. In particular, Sunday schools were a feature in churches that declared Jesus Christ is the Savior of the world and He alone. The first Sunday schools in America were based on memorizing Bible verses and teaching a Bible lesson that taught moral behavior. Singing songs was not an initial feature in the early Sunday schools. As the United States moved west, so did Sunday schools with many developing into churches.

The story is told of a man, possibly in the Baltimore, Maryland area, who had at least one doctorate in theology. The man, possibly named Dr. Matthew, trained men for the pastorate during the week for a living; but on Sundays he taught Sunday school with the children younger than twelve years of age. People told him to stop teaching the children because they were just kids and start teaching the adults. He replied no. "Don't you know that our children are the church of tomorrow? The foundation must be solid!" This man understood the importance of teaching our children! Children are the greatest resource we have and their formation is of the utmost importance!

One of my goals of this book is to persuade you of the critical importance of children's Sunday schools as part of the local church program. I find it helpful to compare the human body to the local church program. The entire Sunday school curriculum should be likened to the skeleton system of the human body. The bones provide structure and give room for our other major organs to work effectively. Without our bones we would be a blob on the floor. Each book of the Bible can be likened to a bone of the body. The people: Adam and Eve, Abraham, Moses, Elijah and Elisha, Mary, Elisabeth, Peter, and Paul become alive to the student because their stories are recorded in the Bible; the most important book for the world. My father, Louis G. Tatter, Jr. was often the Sunday school superintendent in the churches we attended because of his knowledge of education. When I first began teaching Sunday school at the tender age of fourteen, he taught me about the importance of Sunday school. Dad taught that until a person has read and studied under knowledgeable teachers, each book of the Bible, his comprehension of God's message to us would be distorted.

Does your church have a working philosophy regarding the Sunday school ministry? So often the purpose of having a Sunday school is overlooked. Above all else, it has been a powerful tool for evangelism and church growth in the Republic of Chad, Africa since 1981. Take for example the Kyabe area; it was my habit to visit each church in a region that had sent in early January their yearly Sunday school report. These trips took place usually during the spring or Christmas vacation, when the children were home for a week. I had planned to visit the seventeen churches, visiting with at least two every day and thereby finishing within ten days. On arriving, I discovered there were at least twenty-six groups to visit instead of seventeen! Several Sunday school teachers had started classes in neighboring towns over four kilometers (about 2.5 miles) away, so that the children too young (under seven years of age) to walk to their Sunday school class, would also be taught about Jesus. I learned quickly that in the Kyabe region especially, because of the lack of pastors and teachers, a pastor had as many as four churches and I know at least one teacher taught three classes every Sunday! The Kyabe area, within fifteen years, went from seventeen churches to at least twenty seven churches. Why? The children grew up and started their own church in that locality. In several instances the teachers went on to Bible School or Institute to be trained as the pastor. When I left Chad in 2012 there were at least thirty eight Baptist churches in the Kyabe area, all the new ones had developed from having been a Sunday school class! Truly Sunday schools can be a powerful tool of evangelism and church planting!

Who?

My parents were crucial to my success as a missionary in God's service. My parents, Louis Gustav Tatter Jr. and Ruth Louise Edman Tatter always endeavored to take us to church at least every Sunday though sometimes Wednesday night was not possible during the school year because the church at one time was seventeen miles away. They also made sure we had family devotions every day usually at the end of the evening meal, lasting fifteen minutes. Truly my parents understood their responsibility of, "Train up a child in the way he should go: and when he is old, he will not depart from it." Proverbs 22:6! During family devotions my dad would have at least two of us children quote our memory verses learned in Sunday school. This way we would repeat our verse at least three times a week! Little did I know but dad was utilizing the seventh law of teaching-Review! Review! Review! According to John Milton Gregory's Seven Laws of Teaching.

I credit my Christian upbringing as to why, when I was about six years old, I trusted in Jesus Christ to take away my sin and become my Savior. Only Jesus Christ can save a person because of His shed blood on the cross of Calvary. That Sunday morning there was snow on the ground. We were attending an old fashioned Methodist church in Macgregor, Minnesota. Dad was either the principal or the superintendent of the public school. My oldest sister Naomi attended school but I was still too young. Lorna, almost two years younger than me, and I were with Mom and Jennifer, Andrea, Greg and LuAnn had not been born. I distinctly remember sitting in the morning service as the pastor gave the invitation. I realized, Marjorie Louise Tatter, had to make a choice for herself. The fact that Jesus Christ had died for everyone and that I could not depend on the fact my parents were Christians was understood. I had to choose for myself. Even though the pastor gave the invitation I did not go forward. However, the Holy Spirit was making His presence known. Even though it was over sixty years ago, I still remember the heavy burden in my chest. That night as I was getting ready to go to sleep, God made me realize that He loved me so much that even if I was the only person in the world, He would have sent Jesus to die, just for me. What love! I knew I wasn't dying; but the fact that Jesus loved me so much, He would have died just for me pushed me to get up and find my parents. They were in the living room and I told them I had to get saved and would they pray with me. We knelt by my bed and though I don't remember the exact words, I do know Jesus became my Savior that night! How I praise God for Christian parents!

My mother was a registered nurse. One summer, a lady came to stay with us while I was a little girl. My mother explained they had been classmates in nursing school and instead of working in the United States, she worked in Africa as a missionary. I do not remember the lady's name; however, I do remember she was about my mother's height (5'5") and normal size. But I remember how kind, joyous and content she was. She would show me pictures. There was one black and white picture especially of a very small man and woman that was as tall as her waist. The man had a beard and the lady had a tiny baby in her arms. They were very dark people. This lady loved to talk about her people. She told me they were her brother and sister in Christ! She told me they were pygmies and that God loved and died for them just as Jesus died for us. My lasting impression of her was her overwhelming joy in knowing that her life was pleasing to God and her life was making a difference. She is another one of the "who's". Deputation and furlough ministry is vitally important! This is why, when I was on home assignment (commonly called furlough) I asked when reporting to my supporting churches if I could stay with a family instead of staying in a hotel.

Every summer starting from third grade until I graduated from college, I was either a camper, counselor, or camp worker. Sometimes while on furlough I was privileged to serve as the missionary speaker at junior camp. I never refused because while I was junior age, a missionary who served in India made a major impact on my life. Again I don't remember his name but I do remember he was tall and brought a very long snake skin as part of his display. He was our main speaker that week at Camp Lebanon in Minnesota. Not only did he explain our need to be saved but he also spoke on our need to be a "living sacrifice, holy, acceptable unto God, which is our reasonable service." Romans 12:1. Before that time I did not understand that children could be used of God. If memory serves me correctly, that entire week in Bible time this missionary gave examples from the Bible of children God had used! By the last night when it was camp fire time, there were at least four of us who stood up and said we wanted to serve God as a living sacrifice! This missionary is another "who". I am looking forward to heaven when I can thank that missionary for his faithful service!

Another "who" was my pastor Dr. J. Emory Bowker of Gilead Baptist Church in Macon, Georgia. I first heard of Pastor Bowker when he called, asking if I was interested in teaching first grade in what was then

Macon Christian Academy back in the summer of 1975. I was living in northern Minnesota with my parents and babysitting when I received a phone call from him. He had heard that I desired to teach in a Christian school setting and he needed a first grade teacher. Previously I had graduated from St. Cloud State College in Minnesota with a B. S. degree in elementary education and minor in Special education. I had shared with the LORD in my prayer time that I believed in the fundamentals of the faith but I could not defend them with Bible verses. I had told Him that I would like to be able to give an answer for what I believe. I asked the Lord to work it out that I could teach but also get more Bible training. This was the setting when Pastor Bowker called. He was sharing with me the ministries of Gilead Baptist Church in Macon, and I distinctly remember him mentioning they had a Bible Institute program. I asked him more about the program and he said that it was designed for the layman who wanted to be able to give an answer for what he believed! Immediately I knew this was God answering my request! That is how I moved from northern Minnesota to Macon, Georgia back in the summer of 1975!

Pastor Bowker was one of the instructors of the Gilead Bible Institute. Dick Jennings and Jim Sowden were also instructors. I credit Pastor Bowker especially for his teaching of the I AM Bible study method, The Tabernacle, Doctrines of Salvation and the Holy Spirit and Dispensations Courses for helping me stay in Chad thirty-one years. Pastor Bowker also would quiz me on specific doctrines and it was required that I had to substantiate my answers with quoting verses in the Bible! After I was appointed, Pastor Bowker arranged for me to attend several pastor association meetings where I gave my testimony. I praise God for his help because the majority of my supporting churches are in the Georgia, South Carolina area in particular Macon, Augusta, and Atlanta suburbs. It was very hard for a single lady missionary to receive pastor contacts in the south unless they knew exactly what type of ministry you would be doing! I credit Pastor Bowker with helping me tremendously in getting those initial contacts and making me ready to answer the questions pastors were asking.

The next "who" was the next pastor of Gilead as Pastor Bowker died suddenly while on vacation. I was getting ready to return to Chad in a couple weeks when I learned of my pastor dying. I was back in Chad when I heard that Gilead had called Dr. Greg and Ruth Huffman to Gilead. My first impression of them as a couple was that they made a beautiful unit. He persuaded me while on home assignment to teach sixth grade in Gilead's Christian school for one year while I was reporting to my supporting churches. He said there were only seventeen students (fourteen were boys) because he wanted to put before these impressionable young people a person totally consecrated to serving God. Now, twenty-six years later, six, possibly seven of these former students are serving God as either youth or assistant pastors and one missionary. Pastor Huffman also came to Chad as did one of my supporting pastors. This is not easy as travel and living in Chad is physically difficult. They arrived in early March staying eight days in hot weather. My house had no air conditioning only fans but not at night. These men were my first visitors from the states and my Chadian pastors were all excited about meeting my guests. When they learned Pastor Huffman had a doctorate in Bible, they hoped we could arrange a conference for the teachers and pastors lasting four days. I regret working my pastors so hard, but Pastor Huffman and Pastor Bill were beneficial in answering many questions about the local church and teaching biblical geography. I thought it was extremely funny that after leaving Chad, Africa where it was in the low 100's they returned to Atlanta and Macon and immediately a snow storm covered Georgia with snow to cool them down! Thank you again for being such good sports about the heat, Pastors Greg and Bill!

Pastor Greg was also instrumental in my writing not only translating the lessons from French into English but also this book. Both Pastor Greg and Ruth are impressive in their abilities of encouraging believers.

This section of "who" would not be complete unless I mentioned several Chadian people. Pastor Djimouko Edouard, a dentist and pastor, fulfills the JABEZ (I Chronicles 4: 9-10) role in my life. Never will I forget the time when Pastor Djimouko came to Koumra from Sarh and asked me to please come and help the pastors in the Sarh region start Sunday schools for the children in their churches! His wife Elisabeth became one of our Sunday school teachers and a wonderful host when I spent six weeks at their home helping them set up a visitation program for the children in the Banda area. Pastor Djimouko helped much in the training of the Sunday school teachers for the first twenty years of ministry until his death.

Pastor Yamalta Paul was the second Chadian "who". He was the pastor of the Balimba Church where I lived for at least twelve years. He was also the translator for the New Testament into the DAY (pronounced die) language and part of the Old Testament. He was a sounding board regarding the lessons of books four and five of the eight books. I also credit him for encouraging teachers about the translation of the lessons into the tonal national languages with which we worked. I was on home assignment (furlough) when I received the email stating that Pastor Yamalta had died probably of a serious case of malaria.

The next two "who" people are the Ezra and Nehemiah living examples in my life. Pastor Takia Missi Antoine is a modern day Ezra. Roallate Ndoungarou Gedeon is Nehemiah. I first met Pastor Takia when I visited the Kyabe region in January 1982. He was the typist and assistant to the translator of the New Testament in Sara Kaba Naa. After the New Testament was finished, he was sent to the seminary in Cameroon where he eventually received his Master's in Theology. Pastor Takia is now the Director of the Baptist Theological School which resides in Balimba. He is also the president of the Association of Baptist Mid-Missions churches in Chad. Pastor Takia is the Chadian champion of speaking about the importance of reaching our kids and youth for the LORD. He understands the importance of training our children from birth through the teen years! There are at least 350 established Baptist Mid-Missions churches and over 120 more developing. Because of him, the national committee helping the churches train Sunday school teachers, oversee the translation and production of Sunday school teachers has a laymen for President. This president is Roallate Ndoungarou Gedeon. Gedeon has the essential educational background, plus the willingness to be a resource for our Baptist churches. The Baptists have a high school in Sarh that has about fourteen hundred students in grades seven through twelve. Gedeon (Gideon though pronounced Jedeon), is the primary reason for this success. Because of the quality of teaching, this Christian high school is in the top five high schools in the entire country of the Republic of Chad. It has one of the highest standings for graduating seniors. In Chad, students have to pass strict tests before receiving their high school diploma! I will never forget when I returned to Chad for my fourth term of service to learn that Gedeon had requested me to be on the "school board" for the Christian high school. I served until leaving Chad in 2012. Gedeon is highly regarded and helped during the summer months and Christmas vacation, training those who train Sunday school teachers. He teaches the Seven Laws of Teaching superbly! He also speaks English as he worked extensively with Peace Corp workers while a student!

My next "who" is Klah Helene. I first met her when conducting the teacher training workshop for the Bible school students at Maro. Maro is about ten miles north of the Central African Republic and Chad's southern border. I learned she was a widow in her forties with two grown children. While still in Bible school, she was very active in the Sunday school ministry at the Maro Baptist church. After graduating from Bible school she returned to her local church Mayo which is centrally located in the Danamadji/Maro region. She shared with me her plans of walking to all the churches in the Maro/Danamadji area if she could not repair her bicycle. I helped her out and later bought a new bicycle. She found me later with the reports. She travels over 450 miles over very sandy and sometimes rocky roads usually twice a year! She had done this for about ten years! Her main purpose was to encourage the Sunday school teachers in the LORD! She was still doing this when I left Chad though she had developed a disease that causes her hands to shake. She loves working with our children and knows its importance!

My next "who" is actually a couple: Ernest and Elise Difnankai. I met them when they moved to Balimba in 2009 to attend the seminary. Ernest had been a very successful agriculture expert planting trees near the N'djamena area for the purpose of pushing back the Sahara desert. He had found trees that could withstand the harsh climate. However, he and his wife Elise were devout Christians who read their Bible and wanted their life to count for eternity. They remind me of Aquilla and Priscilla in Acts. They enrolled in the seminary and because they understood the importance of reaching and training our children and youth, we grew very close during their years in the theological school. They were Sunday school teachers and Elise especially persevered until she knew all the Sunday school choruses I knew. Ernest took my Sunday school class while I was on home assignment and on Saturday afternoons he worked with youth who had Bibles understanding Wilmington's twelve stages of the Bible which I had translated into French. Ernest Difnankai had also taught how Christ was viewed in each book of the Bible. My last year in Chad, Ernest, while still in school, managed to teach this course at the request of several churches in the Sarh area, with their Sunday school teachers. By the time Ernest graduated, he had prepared a Sunday school program outline not only for children but for all ages in the local church. Ernest graduated as valedictorian of the theological class! It was much easier for me to leave Chad because I knew there was a couple who understood the importance of reaching and training the entire family! I have now learned that

Ernest attended the same graduate Bible school that Pastor Takia had attended and now has his M. Div. I have also learned that in their home church of Guelendeng a special Sunday school class for 4-6 year olds is named Tatter and had about 34 students!

The next "who" is also a Chadian. His name is Kounde Jude. Never will I forget the day we met. I was still living in Koumra and had finished book number 1, printed it, then presented it at the annual Association of Baptist Mid-Missions churches meeting in January. This tall man came and knocked on my door carrying the book of lessons with him. He told me that he lived in N'djamena (capitol of Chad) and during his vacation he wanted to come and talk to me about the Sunday school lessons. (In those days the road to N'djamena was very rough, filled with potholes and usually a two day journey at the least by bus or truck.) Jude told me the lessons were excellent but they would be better if I had pictures with them. I replied that I couldn't agree with him more but I was no artist. He said that he was an artist and designed stamps for the Chadian government and he wanted to draw ink drawings for each one of the new lessons. I told him that I couldn't afford it. He replied that he was volunteering his time and would even provide the paper and ink. He said he wanted to do this as a "ministry to the Lord"! He gave me written permission to use the pictures anyway I desired not requiring any payment! I want to assure you that I gave him a gift every time he presented me with the finished product! The majority of the ink drawings were done by Jude! May God richly bless him! Since books 1, 2 and 3 have been printed and sent at request I have received many remarks as to the quality of the illustrations! They are Kounde Jude's.

The next "who" is Osee Djimasra. Osee (French for Hosea) was instrumental in correcting my French grammar on the books 6 through 8. When my old laptop crashed, he programmed my laptop placing all eight books of lessons plus the training manual in French and in Sara Madjingaye. Thank you Osee! Osee was also a Sunday school teacher from the time he was in tenth grade at the Sarh Christian high school until he went off for nurses training. He later was trained as a workshop director and ended up training Sunday school teachers in the Sarh area!

Finally, my last "who" is Ruth Bekayo. Ruth is a single Chadian lady, cousin of Osee, who wanted to be a Sunday school teacher. She is from the Moundou area. I first met her when she was trained in a workshop and the following year attended the Bible Institute in Balimba. She later was trained as a workshop director, attended the theological school at

Balimba where she graduated the spring of 2017 in Bible. Her passion is teaching and training children.

What?

In this next rather lengthy section, I will not only explain the courses we taught in the teacher training workshops accented with some autobiographical history. The Seven Laws of Teaching or Biblical teaching methods, Child Development: Physically, Socially, Mentally and Spiritually, and Dispensations were the first tier of courses taught. Interspersed were choruses first cataloged by Ruth Bartow and Ada Temple both single ladies with BMM serving chiefly in the Kyabe area when I first arrived in Chad. The second layer of courses taught were the I Am Bible study Method, Best order of activities during the Sunday school hour , Intensive study of Prayer and Sunday school administration. As the "icing' on the course we reviewed general teaching methods especially pertinent to children under fourteen, how to write a letter, and practice teaching. Every student who attended was in a group teaching children starting the second day of the workshop. Generally these practice teaching sessions were with children of a certain age. For instance, the children ages 3-5, were generally one group, the next group were those 6-8, then 9-11, and finally 12 and above. Ideally each student by the end of the week would have taught a new song, reviewed old memory verses, taught the new verse and also taught the new lesson having reviewed the previous Sunday story.

My father was the first person to mention to me The Seven Laws of Teaching by John Milton Gregory LL.D. We never studied them formally but he would introduce a new law while driving to Bemidji, Minnesota. I was about fourteen years old and had just become a Sunday school teacher for pre-primary age children during the summer months as the regular teacher had just given birth to a baby. His informal teaching continued when we moved to Red Lake, Minnesota. I attended school there during my ninth and tenth grades. My Sunday school class grew from three or four kids to at least fifteen children ages 5-8 or 9. By the time we moved to Red Lake, I was the oldest at home as Naomi was in college. Also, Jennifer, Andrea, Gregory and LuAnn had been born with LuAnn being newborn. Teaching children produces overwhelming joy in me.

My years living at Red Lake, Minnesota witnessed a turning point. For the first time I realized what it meant to be a minority. In my high school class of sixty I was the only truly "white" person. The others were Native Americans. I made one good girl friend, Evelyn Loud but we lost contact when I moved to Georgia. She was a Christian who attended the Redby

Mission where we attended and where I taught Sunday school. My sister Lorna and I sang duets in church. One time Lorna and I were asked to sing at a baby's funeral. I thought the baby had died as a result of sickness. However, just before we were to sing, I learned that the baby had frozen to death in the cabin of a truck while the mother was inside the bar getting drunk. As Lorna and I sang behind the pulpit with the small casket immediately in front of us, I broke down sobbing and left. I realized just how sinful and desperately wicked was this world. I told the Lord that I wanted to be used of God to make a difference in my lifetime. I told Him that I would do anything He wanted and would go wherever He directed.

Having studied French in Lausanne, Switzerland with Mademoiselle Péclard for about a year, it was now time to go to the Republic of Chad, Africa. I arrived in N'djamena in mid-December of 1981. When the church in Koumra learned that I had come to work with children, they were enthusiastic. I had heard that every Sunday morning about 7:30 A.M. the children of the Bible school students and the Medical Evangelists and Midwife students would meet together near the Seymour hospital in the public pavilion and some students would take turns teaching them. Never will I forget my first encounter with this group. This building was in a very public place, with a cement floor and an aluminum roof but except for some metal poles, the walls were entirely open. On the floor were some plastic mats and wooden benches. About one hundred children, ages three through early teens, sat on the floor waiting for the lesson. I arrived about fifteen minutes early and soon Pastor Timothy M'solnan, the assistant pastor, brought over a young man and told me that he would translate for me! I was shocked speechless to realize they expected me to teach! I spoke French and the young man translated it into Sara Madjingaye. I asked the Lord, reminding Him I had no audio visual aids, what story should I share? I remember teaching one of my favorite stories from John 6 about the lad who gave his lunch to Jesus and He prayed, blessed the food and started breaking and giving it to the disciples. Over 5000 men, not counting the women and children, were given so much food there were abundant leftovers. My theme was that you do not need to be a "big" person to be used of God. I then mentioned in closing that if anyone wanted to talk with us, to stay behind and we would talk with them individually. Six or seven boys stayed behind that day and trusted in Jesus Christ as their Savior! Later on when they grew up, several of them became Sunday school teachers and having graduated from high school, went on to become pastors or medical evangelists in our churches!

The pastors and deacons came and visited with me and asked what ministry did I suggest starting. I told them we should have a Sunday school for the children. They asked me what kind of people were needed. I replied and still maintain that give me members of church who love children and believe that they can learn and I would help that church. I also told them that we should divide the hundred children into at least three groups as quickly as possible. Except for one, the ladies are still teaching Sunday school! Senior Pastor Kigata Machine brought me eight women and five teenage boys and that was the beginning. By the end of March we had over 300 children in four Sunday school classes and at least half of them had made salvation decisions! Other churches in the Koumra area asked for my help.

We met together either Monday or Tuesday afternoon and I had to write a lesson which we taught. Also I began teaching an abbreviated course of the Biblical teaching methods in particular the Seven Laws of Teaching by John Milton Gregory LL.D. Here is that course: written in paragraph rather than outline form.

The Sunday school teacher is the key. It is vital that he is controlled by the Holy Spirit and that he is walking in faith. In order to have a fruitful ministry, he needs to set goals for his class and have a plan on how to reach them. It is also essential that he loves the children in his class. Children respond to love and respect.

The Sunday school teacher needs to understand and have memorized Matthew 28:19-20, "Go ye therefore, and teach all nations, baptizing them in the name of the Father, and of the Son, and of the Holy Ghost: teaching them to observe all things whatsoever I have commanded you, and, lo, I am with you always, even unto the end of the world. Amen." Children are an integral part of a nation!

It is essential that the teacher see each child as a special creation of God. When I first arrived in Chad, it was obvious that boy children were favored above girl children. Special needs children are just as important as "normal" children. Highly intelligent children should not be favored though they should be challenged to excel.

The Sunday school teacher needs to understand the importance of God adding to the Church by the "foolishness of preaching" (I Corinthians 1:21) and that the teachers are needed for the "perfecting of the body of Christ" (Ephesians 4:11-12).

The Sunday school teacher needs to ask himself these questions daily: does my life glorify God? Is my lesson centered on Christ? And is my lesson taught by the power of the Holy Spirit? Regarding the question of is my lesson centered on Christ, this does not mean that you only teach the Gospel stories of Jesus but during the application you should always mention that only Jesus Christ can save you and He alone.

It is essential that the Sunday school teacher knows he is saved and that Jesus Christ is the master of his life. His faith in God must possess him entirely. His faith in the Bible (2 Timothy 3:16-17) must be unshakeable. His faith in the ministry of teaching and his part in it should motivate him and help him to succeed in his task.

The Sunday school teacher should be well prepared. Because the time with his students is limited, the teacher needs to plan for each minute he has with his class. It is important that he uses this time wisely. It is also essential that he knows how to teach, realizing that this class might be the only contact some of his students may have with God's Word.

No teacher can teach effectively unless he possesses a practical knowledge of all sixty-six books of the Bible. The central theme running through the Bible is Jesus

Christ. Paul referred frequently to Christ as the example we should follow. He emphasized the importance of having a strong spiritual life (Ephesians 5:2, Romans 15:2-3, Philippians 2:15).

The teacher must know his students personally as individuals. He should ask God to help him see one as God sees them. According to I Corinthians 2:14-3:3, everyone is either unsaved (natural man), or a spiritual Christian or carnal Christian. Teachers should desire that all of their students become strong, spiritual Christians. When a child realizes his teacher knows and cares about him, he will be more receptive to what his teacher says.

What is the task of the Sunday school teacher? Every teacher should have well defined goals. His greatest responsibility is to effectively teach the Bible in such a manner that each person in his class desires to be transformed by the grace of God.

It is also his task to introduce Jesus Christ as Savior to his students. First, he needs to discern the spiritual condition of each person in his class. His goal is for each one to be saved and to surrender his life entirely to God. This is his most important responsibility.

It is also the teacher's task to explain to his students how much God loves them and wants to have fellowship with them. He should encourage his students to live an abundant Christian life. God has a plan for each Christian. The Sunday school teacher should use God's Word to guide each student in finding God's will for his life.

It is also the teacher's task to obey the Lord's commandment found in John 21:15 to "feed my sheep." He also needs to encourage his students to "grow in the knowledge of our Lord and Savior" (2 Peter 3:18). He should help each one in his class to develop a strong Christian character as a result of three activities: knowing the Word of God, obeying God's will, and yielding daily to Jesus Christ the LORD.

It is also the task of the teacher to have daily communion with God. Unless a Christian has daily communion with the Lord, it is not possible to grow spiritually. The teacher needs to encourage his students to have daily Bible study and prayer in order to grow in the following areas: worship-the teacher should cultivate the desire in each of his students to set aside time daily to search the Scriptures. The next area is consistent Christian living-it is the responsibility of the teacher to make sure that what is taught in the class is relevant to everyday life. The last area is Christian service-the teacher should excite his students to serve the Lord in his home, school, church, and community. Well do I remember when an eight year old girl in Koumra professed Christ as her Savior the first time she came to Sunday school. Elisabeth and I arranged to visit her home the following Wednesday afternoon having received directions on where she lived. Four days later on Wednesday Elisabeth and I arrived at the quartier named Represantant and saw her looking out the opening in the five foot high grass fence with her mother behind. I remember thinking, "Marji, this lady is going to send you away. Instead, the lady welcomed us into the "compound" and immediately told us that she wanted to know about this "Jesus" because she had witnessed a great change in her daughters' behavior. We led that lady to the Lord and even talked with her husband though he did not accept Christ at that time because he was a Jehovah's Witness." Well do I remember several instances of unsaved parents confessing Christ Jesus as their Savior because they witnessed a genuine change in their child's testimony and behavior!

How does the teacher reach his goals? He needs to have a plan and setting goals are just the beginning, now they must be accomplished. Depending on the age of the group, there are several teaching methods that are good. A variety of methods is best. The best methods for children ages three through twelve years of age is a combination of the following: recitation or memorizing of Bible verses and songs. A child between the ages of five and twelve is better at memorizing than an average adult! The second is teaching Bible stories. A major part of the Bible is written as a narrative and can easily be taught in a story form. It is essential that the teacher is capable of telling a Bible story emphasizing the people, place and action accomplished.

Other teaching methods profitable for the student ten and older are discussions. Discussions are excellent especially for the teen and adults. Another method of teaching is projects. When studying Noah's ark it would be advantageous to make it with popsicle sticks following the model given in Genesis 5-8. Another one when studying the tabernacle of the wilderness is to make a model of the tabernacle placing the furniture in the proper positions.

Another method is research. This is good for teens and young adults who have access to computers that have a good Bible program. Also having a Strong's concordance, and Wilminton's Guide to the Bible are invaluable!

Other methods for those over ten are listening to messages or sermons, attending conferences or seminars!

What are the Seven Laws of Teaching according to Dr. John Milton Gregory, LL.D?

The first law is the law of the teacher. The teacher should know the subject matter of his lesson. He should know even more than what he teaches. Normally a teacher only shares about 30% of what he knows about the particular lesson he is teaching. A teacher who is well prepared will also have better control over his class. A lesson poorly prepared will be poorly taught.

The second law is the law of the student. The student needs to WANT to learn. This is why it is necessary to explain to the students, especially those 7-12 years of age, why the lesson is important for them. The teacher needs to capture the attention of each student, keep his attention, and then excite him to want to know more.

The third law is the law of language. The student must be able to understand what the teacher is saying. The words spoken need to be appropriate for the age level of the students, especially for younger children. In countries where there are multiple languages, such as in Chad, Africa, care needs to be given that the language used is one which the students speak. Teaching someone in a language he does not speak is a waste of time.

The fourth law is the law of the lesson. When a teacher wants to give his students new information, he should start first with what is already familiar and known to them. Jesus did this when He wanted to introduce new concepts. Here are three examples. In John 3, Jesus wanted to explain to Nicodemus that he would one day be lifted up onto a cross and crucified for the sins of the world. This was a new idea, and so he started with an Old Testament story of the brazen serpent on a pole that Nicodemus already knew. In John 3:14, he said," And as Moses lifted up the serpent in the wilderness, even so must the Son of Man be lifted up." The second example was Matthew 12:40, Jesus used the story of Jonah to explain his burial and resurrection. "For as Jonah was three days and three nights in the whale's belly; so shall the Son of Man be three days and three nights in the heart of the earth." Now the third example Jesus was able to help his listeners understand what it would be like in the last days by comparing them to the days of Noah in Matthew 24:37-42.

The fifth law is the law of the process of teaching. This is one of the hardest to implement. The teacher should enthuse, enliven, and guide the student to apply the lesson to his life. He should give just enough to cause the student to search for himself the truths in the Bible. The Sermon on the Mount as well as the entire chapter 6 of John are examples of this law. The teacher should mentally prompt the student by asking him questions for the purpose of enlarging his knowledge.

The sixth law is the law of the process of learning. Learning involves not only the gaining of knowledge but also an action produced because of this knowledge. The lesson has only been successfully taught if the student applies what he has learned to his life. For example, it is not enough just to know that Jesus died on the cross for our sins, we also need to apply this knowledge by accepting and confessing Jesus as our Savior!

The seventh and last law is the law of review and application. Reviewing the lesson and applying it are both essential in order to confirm that the lesson has been understood. Reviewing accomplishes three things: it improves knowledge, it restores and ratifies knowledge and it applies the knowledge to life.

Now we will develop the sixth law: the law of the process of learning a bit further.

The process of learning involves four stages: acquiring, likening, adapting, and applying. The true test of learning is not what the student hears but what he applies to his life. The responsibility of the Christian teacher is to guide his students in this process.

Christian character develops through action. Ignoring what has been taught is just as wrong as not obeying. It is essential that the teacher prepares lessons that are full of activities to help the student apply the truths learned, to his life. Christ put great emphasis on application (Matthew 7:20-24).

There are three aspects to application. The first application concerns the Bible. It is the Word of God that gives us the principles and power to live the Christian life. It is useless to try and change or develop the Christian character independently of biblical instruction. The Bible explains that all are sinners and that the only remedy is Jesus' shed blood. The Bible covers all aspects of life-sports, social activities, the home, school, and the church. It is important for Christian teachers to emphasize that the Bible provides the answers to all the problems of this world!

The next application concerns the teacher. No one can teach a biblical truth unless he has first become like a child and humbly applied it to his own life (Matthew 18:1-6). Jesus taught the importance of humility when he washed his disciples' feet in John 13:1-20. Application is important for understanding. Peter often heard Jesus teach about the importance of forgiveness (Matthew 6:5, 18:21-22); but it was not until Christ forgave him after Peter's denial that he finally understood the concept (Luke 22:61-62).

The next complex application concerns the student. The goal of the teacher is to present the lesson in such a way that the student will see the need to apply what he has learned. Keeping this in mind, the teacher should seek new and different ways to help the student learn several important truths.

The first truth is salvation. It is necessary that each child understand that he is personally responsible to receive Jesus Christ as his Savior and Lord. No one else can make that decision for him.

The next truth is spiritual growth. The teacher should help his students who are Christians know how to acquire spiritual disciplines that will help them grow in their faith. Learning how to pray and study the Bible should be taught systematically.

The next truth is stewardship. The spiritual development of each child includes learning how to be a good steward. He needs to learn the importance of the giving of his time and finances to the church. He needs to learn that everything belongs to God and that he needs to use wisely what God has entrusted to his care. In Sunday school, each child should learn to give liberally, systematically, and joyfully!

The last important truth concerns service. An adequate and well taught Sunday school program will help each student use his talents in service to the Lord. A wise teacher will seize each occasion to show the children how to serve in the home- a child should first act as a Christian at home. In his church-a student should learn how to serve in his local church. In his school and neighborhood-a child needs to learn how to be a witness to those around him. In the world-it is the church's responsibility to spread the Gospel to the world. Well do I remember while living in Balimba the theological student and I were visiting the boy who had been saved in Sunday school. We were outside and the junior age boy was answering our questions. We noticed this older man who was building a dried mud brick wall listening closely. He stopped and came over to tell us that he knew his nephew had changed because when told to go and buy cigarettes for the uncle the boy remarked politely," I'm sorry, but I cannot buy them for you because I am now a Christian and cigarettes are bad for you." This boy was living for Christ!

What should the teacher wear? The teacher should dress modestly and appropriately. He should be clean; hair, jewelry, and accessories should not be a distraction. A specific uniform is recommended in some countries, but I am not in favor of this because there is no biblical basis found for this teaching in the New Testament.

The Sunday school teacher should exercise self-control. The majority of Sunday school teachers desire that God will work in the lives of their students and transform them so that they are tranquil and attentive in class. However, a spirit-filled teacher is capable of manifesting the Fruit of the Spirit (Galatians 5:22-23). Even in difficult circumstances the teacher should remain calm and composed. One time when I was teaching in a building with a grass thatch roof, a snake started descending from the roof and I had to quickly and calmly cause the children to leave the building while another person killed the snake with the "koutou de jeu". (a metal instrument curved like half a paper clip but much larger).

The second course I taught in the Republic of Chad, Africa was a child development course. Why was this course necessary? Because I found many adult nationals, especially adult men, who thought that children were miniature adults! Except for medical evangelists, midwives, and educators, I learned that the nationals had very little knowledge of how a child thought and developed! How glad I was for my training as a licensed elementary educator! I thank the LORD for a great child development professor at St. Cloud State University in St. Cloud, Minnesota who made us think and learn! The LORD helped me develop a course which I call a brief overview of childhood psychology and development.

What is psychology? It is the scientific study of the soul. In the training program, we briefly study childhood development in the areas of physical, mental, social, and spiritual growth from birth until eighteen years of age. Generally speaking it is important when studying the development of children to realize that children are naturally curious and they need to know WHY something is important before they will apply it to themselves.

It is also necessary to realize that childhood is divided into three general periods: birth to three years, four to six years, and finally seven to eleven years. It is so important for steady, physical growth for a young child (birth to three years old) to eat sensibly and regularly.

Socially, a child needs to be in a regular family setting with at least one person always available with whom he feels secure. He needs a regular routine with enough activities that challenge him physically, mentally, socially, and spiritually. By the time a child is three years old, it is important that he is in contact with others his age for several hours a day.

How does language develop in a person? It develops quickly during childhood. By the time he is 18 months to two years old, a child may ask for something to drink by saying, "Water," or "Drink." From two to four years, a child may use a short phrase such as "Water, mama." By the time he is four years old, he should be able to construct a complete sentence like, "Mama, please give me a drink of water."

By the age of three, a child is egocentric. In other words, he thinks the world revolves around him and that his parents belong to him. He sees things in general (globalism) and not the individual details. As a child grows older, he distinguishes details. For example, a three-year-old just sees a tree. Later, he can distinguish leaves, branches, and trunk.

A child reacts favorably to colors, shapes, and bright patterns. A variety of activities is necessary to challenge him intellectually. It is of primary importance that each child realizes that he is valuable as a person. He must understand that he is a special creation of God!

I Samuel 2:26, "And the child Samuel grew on, and was in favor both with the LORD, and also with men." This key verse was memorized by every teacher in training! Some day if the LORD tarries I hope to write a book about all the children under eighteen years old God used in the Bible. In the meantime we are going to briefly study how a child develops from the time he is born until he is eighteen years old.

Physically, the normal child from the time he is born until his fourth birthday, grows rapidly and starts to walk at around one year of age. He is not capable of dressing alone before the age of three. He is totally dependent on parents or caregiver during the first year. He starts to verbalize noises at about five months of age; short phrases appear at about 17 or 18 months.

Mentally, the normal child does not have robust health, but is able to follow a short program of simple exercise. He has an imagination and an attention span of about five to eight minutes. He does not understand time except for night/day or light/dark. He is affectionate and develops well mentally in a positive environment. He is capable of understanding good and bad and can learn short verses and songs after two years of age.

Socially, the normal child in this age group is capable of learning and experiencing new activities within the family. He enjoys playing in small groups (2-3) by the age of two. He thinks the world revolves around him; needs to learn to share. He starts to learn to like and to please.

Spiritually, the normal child is able to worship God sincerely. He starts to understand the reality of God and that God loves him. He is able to understand that disobedience is sin. He is naturally capable of trusting someone within a nurturing environment.

I Samuel 2:26, "and the child Samuel grew on, and was in favor both with the LORD, and also with men." The next age group to study is the child between the ages of four and six. Have you successfully memorized 1 Samuel 2:26? Notice the verse emphasizes Samuel's relationship first with the LORD.

Physically, the normal child between four and six years old is better able to work alone. He can get dressed and is prone to talk constantly. He has periods of anger and feels the need to defend himself. He does not have great physical resistance and is inclined to colds.

Mentally, the child between 4 and 6 has an attention span that has increased to around 12 minutes. He has a good imagination but still does not have a clear understanding of time. He learns easily in a caring environment. His mental capacity grows rapidly at this time. He learns best by concrete examples. He is capable of learning longer verses. He is able to learn and understand new experiences both emotionally and spiritually.

Socially, the child in this 4-6 age bracket is able to adapt to new social experiences. He is able to distinguish different ways of speaking to people. He is able to play simple games in small groups. He can learn to respect authority if taught at a young age. He is still egocentric and needs to learn to share with others. He enjoys pleasing people but also enjoys talking. He begins to exhibit behavior of leadership and wants to please people. He enjoys acting out stories.

Spiritually, this child of 4-6 years of age continues to worship God sincerely. Lessons on Creation are profitable at this time. He speaks personally to God and understands that God loves him and cares for him if he is raised in a godly home. He understands that disobedience is sin, but that God provides for all needs. He needs to understand the importance of placing confidence in God and obeying Him.

I Samuel 2:26,"and the child Samuel grew on, and was in favor both with the LORD, and also with men." The child between the ages of seven and nine is our next group to study.

Physically, the normal child of this age grows less rapidly. He slows down. He is prone to periods of intense energy that is followed by fatigue. He is still prone to colds and other contagious illnesses. He needs a variety of activities that are well explained.

Mentally, the normal child this age can get emotionally involved and is able to make comparisons. He has a need to be guided as well as loved. He is imaginable, reasonable, and credible. If he can read, the knowledge of the outside world enlarges. He can understand better if historical and geographical differences are explained. He especially enjoys biblical stories that exhibit the power of God. He starts to solve his own problems verbally. He is capable of discrimination and wants to make his own decisions. He is still better at memorizing words rather than ideas.

Socially this child at this age of 7-9 years of age seeks new people to get to know him. He needs to learn how to help, be kind, to cooperate, and to be generous. He imitates trusted and loved adults and seeks their approval. He plays with peers and desires his own pet. He enjoys stories about children but reacts negatively against unreasonable stories. He is not yet interested in competition; wants to choose friends but does not yet seek a best friend for life.

Spiritually this child finds helpful, lessons or stories that illustrate spiritual maturity. He is capable of understanding accountability and that God forgives sin. He learns to respect authority by teaching and by example. He needs to learn to pray and to live for Jesus Christ. He can learn that the Bible has the answer to every problem and the importance of reading and understanding it. He needs to learn that sin should be confessed immediately. In Chad sixty-two percent of children who attended Sunday school made salvation decisions when they were seven years old; twenty-six percent were six years old. Rarely were children making salvation decisions under six or older than ten!

I Samuel 2:26, "and the child Samuel grew on, and was in favor with the LORD, and also with men." The child between the ages of ten and twelve years old is next.

Physically, the normal child of this age is typically the healthiest in his life. He is also naturally active and excitable. He desires independence; is not naturally neat or orderly! He enjoys outdoor activities and needs daily exercise; likes sports and adventure. He grows at a moderate rate.

Mentally, this average child memorizes easily. He does not like criticism but understands corrective conversations. He understands time and space as well as problems that concern him. He enjoys new assignments if they are meaningful. He is capable of many interests and exhibits creativity in finding solutions. He enjoys stories involving nature and brave people. He can concentrate longer and enjoys collecting objects and explaining their benefits.

Socially, this typical child is easily engaged in activities yet desires an impartial engagement. He enjoys being part of a peer group and taking part in a lesson. He enjoys playing with children of like gender and is not yet interested in the opposite sex. He is prone to idolize those he respects. He is not as timid and enjoys competition. He also expresses sympathy for hurting people. He starts to compare people and notices differences in them.

Spiritually, he is ripe for salvation. He is learning to grow in Christ is essential for spiritual growth. He can also understand basic doctrines such as the Holy Spirit indwelling the believer. Visuals while teaching are still helpful. He needs to be encouraged to spend time daily in studying God's Word. He is highly interested in others, and it is important that his family is saved. He has a solid faith and asks important questions. He is capable of digging deeply and understanding basic principles. He can appreciate spiritual values.

I Samuel 2:26, "And the child Samuel grew on, and was in favor with the LORD, and also with men." The child between thirteen and eighteen years old is the last group we study psychologically.

Physically, the average child grows rapidly and in spurts. It is possible for a boy to gain more than twenty pounds in a year. Boys may also grow 5 inches in one year for several years; girls generally less. Heart, lungs, bones, and muscles develop proportionately. Girls reach their physical maturity before boys. They are embarrassed about being clumsy due to growth spurts. The energy levels at times vary from too much energy to not having any energy. It is the most tumultuous time of life; they are intensely interested in sex.

Mentally, the typical child can memorize easily. Their development is more rapid and complex than ever before. He tends to be proud of accomplishments. His sense of humor is well developed and if not guided, can be cruel. He daydreams about being a hero. He reacts emotionally to things that are important. He demands to be allowed to make his own decisions regarding his personal life.

Socially, the normal child is more aware of the world than past generations due to modern technology. He is capable of trusting not just family but also leaders in the church and school. He is talkative and follows a peer group. Though he acts as if he is indifferent, he seeks new experiences. He abhors being considered a child. He is intensely attracted to the opposite sex. He needs to be considered important or essential to other people.

Spiritually, the normal person of thirteen to eighteen is in the company of older young people for the purpose of being guided by them. He is preoccupied by "What? Who? Why am I here? How?" He needs to know the LORD Jesus Christ and have assurance of salvation. He should be actively involved in church work. He needs to be valued and to have the guidance of trusted church leaders.

Thus ends the second course. The next course is the course of Dispensations.

When I first arrived in the Republic of Chad, we did not teach this course of Dispensations. Yes, I spoke, wrote, and read French, but at the most only 4 out of 10 Chadians could speak French. Of course, we had the entire Bible in French but when only 4 out of 10 people could read the entire Bible it was hard for me to understand. There was a New Testament in the Sara Madjingaye and Day(pronounced dye)languages but not the entire Bible. Because I make it a priority of mine to be reading the Bible systematically starting in Genesis and reading through Revelation I understood how important it was to have the entire Bible in their languages. One of my precious memories consists of training the wives of both the Bible Institute as well as the theological students how to be a Sunday school teacher. The memory of seeing the ladies bring their well-used New Testaments to class is memorable. When they finished their course they asked me to continue praying that soon they would have the whole Bible in Sara Madjingaye and Day because the stories of Adam and Eve and Moses are not found in the New Testament!

When we first conducted the week long training class I needed to find someone who could give a basic overview of the entire Bible. Naively, I thought the pastors of the respective churches who had sent their students to be trained as Sunday school teachers would arrange classes in their respective churches to teach a more in-depth course in French called "Walk through the Bible." Each pastor had been taught this course in their Bible Schools. I thought a brief outline taking five or six hours would suffice. The teacher taught for five hours but he never got out of Genesis! The second week long training session, Francois Nguindet, a highly gifted medical evangelist at Balimba, taught a modified course of Dispensations. This course was so necessary because we did not just teach the stories found in the Gospels and Acts but also the stories in the Old Testament. I knew the importance that our teachers, who, for the most part, had never read the entire Bible let alone the New Testament, needed to understand the treasure we have which is the Bible.

The first week long training workshops had to be conducted in French as that was the only language I knew besides English. We Baptist Mid-Missions missionaries in Chad worked with approximately nine different language groups; but about 43% of the Chadian people in the beginning, spoke, wrote, and read French. The majority of those trained were young high school men. It is my experience that women understand children ages 3-6 better than men. But the majority of women could not read French and only had the New Testament in their language. It was rare to find a teacher who had ever read the entire Bible, starting in Genesis and ending in Revelation. Just before I left Chad, we compared how many men and women had been trained in our workshops during the 31 years. There were at least 875 men who were trained compared to only 240 women.

I was first introduced to Dispensations when I attended the Gilead Bible Institute in 1975. It was suggested that we read the correlating Bible passage for each dispensation. I did this, and it helped tremendously. I would recommend anyone who took this course to do the same. When we were training the new teachers, we did not require this during the workshop; but we suggested that they do this on their own after the workshop ended. We gave extensive notes but did not read each reference because of insufficient instructional time.

The course of Dispensations was never taught by me unless there were only women in the class. Only twice did I teach the course of Dispensations. I was always blessed to find a pastor who was a great teacher and who could teach this as well as the course on prayer. I will always be grateful to Francois Nguindet, Djako

Moise, and Takia Missi Antoine who so effectively taught this course!

In the Gilead Bible Institute as part of the final test, I had to verbally explain a detailed wall chart on the seven dispensations. I greatly regretted never finding a similar chart in French. It has always been my hope that a wall chart could be made available while teaching this course.

By far, the courses of Dispensations as well as Sunday school Administration were the hardest courses for our students to grasp. I discovered that women had a hard time understanding the overall concept of the Bible. But they made up for this lack with the courses on child development and the practical courses! The reason the study of dispensations is necessary is complex.

Dispensations' teaches that God always has a specific requirement for people to complete. When they fall, He has to send judgment. A Bible period is taught distinctively according to its dispensation. The principle people of each dispensation are mentioned and therefore their actions are better understood. The fact that God is vitally interested in man and that everything He promises will eventually be accomplished is evident. Finally, the covenants normally should be taught in an expanded workshop but at least the references are given in the course.

The Greek word for Dispensations is "oikokonomia." In some passages it is translated differently. In Luke 16:2-4 it is translated "stewardship." In I Corinthians 9:17, Ephesians 3:2 and Colossians 1:25 it is stated as dispensation.

A dispensation is defined as the manner that God administers the concerns or business of men. This definition presumes three things: the intervention of God to know what each man needs, each man has the responsibility to submit to God's requirements, and there is a period or "age" during which man is to accomplish God's requirements.

Regarding salvation, before the cross, man was saved by looking toward the day the Messiah Jesus Christ, would come and become the sacrifice for our sins and ultimately rise from the grave. Grace has always been present. Since Christ's death, burial, and resurrection; man is saved by faith by believing in Christ and His finished work on the cross. Here are other examples of people who were saved by faith: Abraham-Romans 4:4, Abel-Hebrews 11:4, Enoch-Hebrews 11:5, Noah-Hebrews 11:7, Isaac, Jacob-Hebrews 11:9, Sarah-Hebrews 11:11, Joseph-Hebrews 11:22, Moses-Hebrews 11:23-26, Joshua-Hebrews 11:30, Rahab-

Hebrews 11:31, Church age believers-Ephesians 2:8,9.

There are seven dispensations: Innocence, Conscience, Human Government, Promise, Law, Church or Grace, and Millennium. Each dispensation is characterized by 1) A new position for man, 2) New privileges and responsibilities for man that are revealed at the beginning of each new dispensation 3) Man's disobedience followed by divine judgment.

The dispensation of Innocence's biblical period is described in Genesis 1:1 through 3:24. We do not know how many years this dispensation lasted. It starts with the creation of man and ends with Adam and Eve being chased from the Garden of Eden. The fall of man is part of this dispensation. The beginning of this dispensation was the creation of the man and woman (Genesis 1:26-27).

Man's responsibility during this time was to be fruitful and multiply; to replenish and subdue the earth; and to have dominion over the fish, cattle, and everything that creeps upon the earth (Genesis 1:28-29). Man was to eat the fruit of the trees.

The test that God assigned to man was that they could eat of any tree of the garden except of the Tree of Knowledge of good and evil (Genesis 2:16-17). The consequence of eating of that tree was that they would surely die (Genesis 2:17). They disobeyed when Eve took of the tree and ate and then gave to Adam who also ate (Genesis 3:6).

In Genesis 3:14-21 we find the judgment on this dispensation. The serpent, who had been indwelt by Satan: was cursed and would have to crawl on his belly; the Redeemer would come and defeat him. On the woman: childbirth would be painful; her desire would be toward her husband. On the man: the soil of the earth would be cursed; work would be difficult. This dispensation ends with man (Adam and Eve) being chased from the Garden of Eden (Genesis 3: 23-24).

The second dispensation is called Conscience and its biblical period is described in Genesis 3:22-Genesis 8:13. This dispensation begins with man knowing good and evil (Genesis 3:22) and ends with the flood (Genesis 8:14). ANOTHER NAME FOR THIS PERIOD IS THE Dispensation of Moral Responsibility. According to Ussher, the length of this dispensation is about 1800 years. During this dispensation, man was to be guided by his conscience.

This dispensation started in Genesis 3:22 with the knowledge of good and evil. Mans responsibility was to offer blood sacrifices for sin. (Genesis 4:4-5) The test was for man to act according to his conscience in choosing good and rejecting evil (Genesis 3:22). The consequence of man's sin was that God decided to destroy the earth (Genesis 6:6-7).

Man's disobedience was multiple. Cain refused to offer a blood sacrifice and killed his brother Abel (Genesis 4:7-16). Man's wickedness was so great that God decided to destroy everyone except Noah and his family (Genesis 6:1-11).

The judgment was the sending of the flood that destroyed everything except those in the ark and the animals in the seas (Genesis 6:13-7:24). God gave us the rainbow to remind us that He would never destroy the earth with a universal flood.

The end of this dispensation was the flood that covered the whole earth (Genesis 7-8:13). Noah and his family were in the ark about a year!

The third dispensation is called Human Government and its biblical period is described in Genesis 8:15 – Genesis 11:32. The third dispensation lasted about 400 years. It starts in Genesis 8:15 with Noah and his family leaving the ark and it ends, in Genesis 11:32 with the confusion of languages at the Tower of Babel. All types of food, including meat, were allowed to be eaten. The principle people in the dispensation are Noah, his sons Shem, Ham, and Japheth, and their wives.

This dispensation begins after the flood (Genesis 8:16). After Noah left the ark, he built an altar to offer sacrifices to God. God used the symbol of a rainbow to seal a covenant with Noah (Genesis 9:14-16).

Man's responsibility was to govern the land. Murder was prohibited and was punishable by death. Man was also to multiply and replenish the earth (Genesis 9:1-7). The test involved governing and the caring out of punishment for the guilty (Genesis 9:6), as well as obeying the commandment to replenish the earth.

The consequence involved the protection of human life. Until Christ comes back and reigns on the earth, government is foremost to protect life (Genesis 9:6). Their disobedience was the building of the Tower of Babel. Instead of replenishing the earth, they all stayed together in the land of Shinar (Genesis 11:1-4). Their hearts were filled with pride and they decided to try to reach heaven to make a name for themselves.

Their judgment is found in Genesis 11:7. The Lord descended and confounded their language. Before this time, they all spoke the same language! He did this to cause them to disperse throughout the earth.

The end of this dispensation was the confusion of languages (Genesis 11:7).

The fourth dispensation is Promise; its biblical period is recorded in Genesis 12:1 through Exodus 18:27. According to Ussher, this dispensation also lasts about 400 years. God works primarily through Abraham and his descendants during this time.

The dispensation of Promise begins with the call of Abraham in Genesis 12:1. God instructs him to leave his country and go to a place that God would show him. He promises to make Abraham a great nation. Other nations who treated Abraham's nation well would be blessed and vice versa (Genesis 12:3).

The test for the dispensation of Promise: Abraham was to leave his home in Ur of the Chaldeans. He was to go to the land that God would give him (Genesis 12:1-2). Abraham's responsibility: he was to obey God by going. He was to develop and occupy the Promised Land (Genesis 12:1-2).

The consequences: God's covenant with Abraham and his descendants concerning the possession of the land of Canaan was everlasting and unconditional (Genesis 17:7-8). Abraham and his descendants were to keep God's covenant by practicing circumcision of the males (Genesis 17:9-14).

Their disobedience: Abram abandoned the land God had given him (Genesis 12:10). Sarai did not believe in the promise given by God (Genesis 16:2). Abram took Hagar the Egyptian as his wife in order to have a son (Genesis 16:4). The Israelites murmured and complained (Exodus 14:11-12, 15:24). Except for Joshua and Caleb, the Israelites refused to enter the Promised Land (Numbers 13:31-32).

The judgment: The Israelites were slaves in Egypt for about 400 years. All of the Israelites over the age of 20 except Caleb and Joshua would die in the wilderness and not be allowed to enter the Promised Land (Numbers 14:29). This dispensation ended with slavery in Egypt.

The fifth dispensation is Law; its biblical period is recorded in Exodus 20 through Acts 2 and Revelation. The Dispensation of Law starts with the giving of the Ten Commandments to Moses on Mount Sinai. It ends temporarily with Christ ascending into heaven and the arrival of the Holy Spirit in Jerusalem (Acts 2:1). The majority of the Old Testament falls into this dispensation. The Dispensation of the Church (sometimes called Dispensation of Grace) is a parenthesis that starts at the end of the gospels. I personally believe it begins with the arrival of the Holy Spirit in Jerusalem (Acts

2:1), and it will end with the rapture of the Church (I Thessalonians 4:13-17, Revelation 4:1). The Great Tribulation is a return of the Dispensation of Law. The Sabbath will be reinstated during the seven years of the tribulation.

The beginning of the Dispensation of Law starts at Mount Sinai, when God gives Moses the Ten Commandments and the design for the tabernacle (Exodus 20). The Israelites had the responsibility to offer sacrifices before God (Leviticus 1-7: 16). The test (Deuteronomy 6:5-6; 28:14 and Leviticus 26:14-39); they were charged to love the Lord their God. They were to practice all the given laws and commandments.

Their disobedience is recorded in many passages. The following references are but a few: Daniel 9:8-19, 2 Chronicles 36:16; and Isaiah 30:9.

The judgment of the Dispensation of Law: the kingdom was divided (I Kings 11:11-12). They were taken into captivity (I Kings 14-15). Israel was dispersed (Nehemiah 1:8).

The end of the dispensation: The death of Jesus Christ; the dispersion of the nation of Israel; and Great Tribulation or seventieth week of Daniel. (Daniel 12)

The sixth is the Dispensation of the Church and its biblical period starts in Acts 2 through Revelation 4. Since the death of Jesus and the arrival of the Holy Spirit, a new responsibility is given to both Jews and Gentiles. A Gentile is anyone who is not a direct descendant of Isaac, son of Abraham. This responsibility is personal, in that each person must recognize that he is a sinner. However, by believing on the shed blood of Jesus Christ and receiving him as Savior, anyone can be saved.

This dispensation began on the Day of Pentecost with the baptism of the Holy Spirit (Acts 1:5; 2:1-4; and Acts 10:15-17). Man's responsibility in this dispensation is that everyone is to believe in Jesus who was sent by God the Father (John 6:29). We are currently living this dispensation.

The test is that he that believes already has eternal or everlasting life and is born of God (John 3:18, 36; 5:24: Romans 10:9; and I John 5:1).

The consequences of not believing in Jesus Christ and in him alone are that one has already been judged and that the wrath of God abides on him (John 3:18; 3:36; and Ephesians 2:12).

The judgment of this dispensation is recorded in Revelation 20:4; Romans 1:24-32; Revelation 6:16-21; and Revelation 10:10.

The seventh and last dispensation is the Dispensation of the Millennium; its biblical period is Revelation 19:11-20:15. In this dispensation, Christ will return to earth and establish himself as ruler over all the earth. He will reign from the throne of David in Jerusalem for 1000 years. Peace will finally rule over the entire world!

The beginning of this dispensation starts with a blood bath in Revelation 19:11. After this battle called Armageddon, Christ will start to reign in Jerusalem. Satan is bound at this time. During this time, those who were saved during the Church Age will reign with Christ on earth for 1000 years (Revelation 20:4-60).

Those tested during this dispensation are those who will be born during these 1000 years. They will need to believe in Jesus Christ in order to be saved (Revelation 20:12).

The disobedience is recorded in Revelation 20:8 when Satan is loosed and some will follow him. Their judgment will take place at the Great White Throne. There, Jesus will judge Satan and the unbelievers.

They will then be thrown into the Lake of Fire (Revelation 20:10).

We encourage the teachers to read through the Bible starting with Genesis 1 and marking in their Bibles the different Dispensations. Of major importance is remembering the Gospels were written at the end of the dispensation of law and Acts marks the beginning of the dispensation of the church. My pastor, Dr. Emory Bowker always cautioned us to remember the beginnings and endings of the dispensations showed much transition. This is why Acts must be remembered as a transitional book. This ended the simplified course of Dispensations.

The next group of courses taught in our workshops helps reinforce the foundational studies and activities of the Sunday school.

The next course we taught our teachers was a plan of how to utilize the hour most beneficially devoted to Sunday school for children. Keep in mind this hour was likely the only time children from three years old up received any kind of religious instruction geared to their age for a week.

When preparing for Sunday school, there are several things to take into consideration. First, it is necessary when working with children under the age of seven, to plan for and provide enough time for them to get rid of the "wiggles." It is also important to pick songs that reinforce the theme of the lesson. Although Chadian children love to sing, it may be necessary to limit the singing time. We found that if we sang more than one song with the older children then we did not have adequate time to teach the verse. I would also highly recommend allowing the children who bring a Bible to read the text for the lesson. We want to encourage our children to read God's Word!

I found it essential during the course of the workshop to provide a plan that the teachers could follow. Here is the order that I would recommend: first learn a new song. This can be started before Sunday school with the children who come early. We learn a new song because the children love to sing and this song likely motivates them to come earlier. This new song becomes a positive reinforcement that helps them spiritually.

The second activity is to pray no longer than one or two minutes. This should be kept short. One time I attended a class where the teacher had forty children in his class. He prayed for each one of the children by name and it took twenty minutes. The children were all under seven years of age and he lost control of his class. Praying quiets and calms the children. It is especially important to teach them how to bow their heads and fold their hands. Remember, we want our children to pray. It is best if the teacher prays with the small ones. Incidentally, I suggested to the teacher after Sunday school ended that it was great he knew all the children's names. But it was better he prayed a short prayer because of time restraints and when at home during the week he could pray for each individual.

After the short prayer we again sing songs that are familiar to the students. This should be kept short- three or four minutes is sufficient. Singing helps the children learn new things and it also helps them remember the things they have already learned (4th law of teaching).

The next activity is reviewing previously learned verses. At least five minutes should be taken. The goal is that the children recognize at least four of the previously learned memory verses by their reference and immediately be able to quote them. Have the children quote the verses together before specifically choosing one child to say them. Memorizing verses helps the children to meditate on them (Psalm 119:9-11).

The fifth activity, taking at the most 2 minutes, is to sing the new song taught to the early arrivals. It is good to sing the new song at this time, especially with the younger children. With children 8 years and older, this is not as necessary but it is beneficial.

The sixth activity is learning the new memory verse. This should take about 4 minutes. This verse should relate to the theme of the lesson. This is especially important for younger children. If you use the lessons in our eight books, the Bible memory verse is chosen for you. In countries where several languages are spoken, the children under 8 years of age should learn the verse in their mother tongue!

The seventh activity is explaining the new verse. At the most, this should only take two to three minutes. This explanation should take place immediately after the children have memorized the verse and quoted it together twice. The key words as well as unknown words should be explained or defined. After the explanation, it is important to quote the verse together twice. This verse should previously have been written on the board for the children to read. A good way to help them memorize the verse is to alternate between erasing a few of the words and quoting the verse. Continue until only the reference is visible!

The eighth activity is especially necessary for the under eight years old class. It is an action song. By this time, particularly the younger children need to get up and move around. Action songs like "My God is so big", Deep and Wide", and "This Little Light of Mine" are ideal for this activity.

The ninth activity is the review of the previous lesson. This should last 2-3 minutes. The best way to review is to show the picture from the previous lesson and ask the children questions about it. The younger children should be able to identify the people in the story and tell where it is found in the Bible. Those older than nine years old might be able to retell the story. I had one boy who, when he was only 8, could recite in order all the miracles of Elijah and Elisha and where they were found in the Bible! Again, this activity is the 4th law of teaching, of going from what is known to what is new.

The tenth activity is prayer by the teacher who teaches the new story. This should last no more than one minute. This time of prayer is important for the teacher who is telling the story. Also, I always made sure that the children bowed their heads and closed their eyes. This had a calming effect on them.

The eleventh activity is the new lesson or Bible story. This should last about 15-20 minutes for the older student and less than 15 for the younger students. The new lesson is placed near the end of the hour because we want the children to reflect and meditate on the Bible story when they leave. It is a psychological fact that what is taught at the end is more likely to be remembered. It is important that the children know that the lesson comes from the Bible.

I always taught with my Bible in hand and my notes nearby. When possible, I tried to have the children read at least one verse from their Bible. The first Bible I ever received had a colorful cover and was a gift from my church when I turned seven. One habit my parents instilled in us was to always bring our Bibles to church.

If the children were too young to read from the Bible, I asked them to listen carefully for the following information: who the people in the story were, where they were, what happened, when it happened, and how it happened. This activity develops comprehension!

To help the children understand and remember the Bible story, I would wait a few minutes before I showed any pictures. I had learned that if you showed the pictures immediately at the beginning of the lesson, the children did not listen or remember all details to the story. If possible, I wrote important information on the chalkboard and tried to have maps and other visual aids hanging on the walls.

It is important that time be allowed for children to make personal decisions such as for salvation or confession of sin at the end of the lesson.

The next activity is the taking of the offering. This should take at the most 1-2 minutes. It is also possible to have this at the beginning of the hour, so that children do not play with their offering and get distracted during the lesson.

Offerings are necessary. They teach the children the importance of giving back to God what He has given to them. Even a child can learn the importance of stewardship!

The next activity is the final prayer lasting 1-2 minutes. Part of the reason why we had this final prayer time was to encourage the children to learn to pray daily. Especially with the younger children, we often prayed "The Believers Model Prayer" (Matthew 6:9-13). I would make sure all the children had bowed their heads and closed their eyes and had their hands folded. Then we would say it together. Sometimes with the older children I would ask for a volunteer. When they had finished I would thank him.

The last activity generally was the blessing. In Chad, it is usual for the teacher to say a blessing in his prayer asking the Lord to keep the children safe during the week before they came back the next Sunday. I simply prayed and asked the Lord to bless and keep each person and help them to serve the Lord. I also stayed for several minutes after class to be available in case the children had a question or wanted me to pray with them.

During the course of the workshop we would practice teach ideally with children divided into several groups. Ideally the classes were no more than twenty students in a class but this was not always possible, especially with the younger child ages three through five.

The next or fifth course, the I AM Bible Study Method is essential for every serious Sunday school teacher and my favorite course to teach. Why? Because learning how to encourage myself in the LORD is the chief reason I was able to stay in CHAD 31 years. Living in CHAD was hard but I love the people not the country. I want to thank my first pastor, Dr. J. Emory Bowker for introducing and teaching this method to me back in 1975. It was part of the Gilead Bible Institute course SPIRITUAL LIFE.

There are four disciplines or responsibilities of the spiritual Christian. The first one is to meditate the Bible. Some of my favorite references for this discipline are: Joshua 1:7-9; Psalm 1:1-3, 119:9-11, 49, 129 and many others. Memorizing Bible verses is crucial as many children never possess a Bible until they are in their teens, if then. When they memorize they can meditate on the verses. I know one teacher who memorized the entire 119th Psalm (176 verses)!

The next discipline is prayer. I Thessalonians 5:17, Philippians 4:6-7, Jeremiah 33:3 and many others, commands us to pray. When I first started in Chad the majority of the new teachers thought prayer was to ask only for things like good health, nice clothes etc! This is why there is a special course on prayer in the workshop.

The third discipline or responsibility is to witness in word and deed. Matthew 28:19-20, 5:13-16, John 20:21, Mark 16:15, Acts 1:7-11 all reveal this command. In regards to Matthew 5:13-16, I must insert a true story as to its importance. In 1985 during the Christmas holiday of 10 days I was asked to conduct a workshop in the Danamadji area of Chad. My team and I arrived and I was delighted to find several ladies amongst the group we were training. But one young lady troubled me because she mentioned that she lived for Jesus during the day but what she did at night was no one's business. I should have written a note to her pastor but did not. She finished the weeklong course, passing the tests and returned to her church as did the other people we trained. About 6 months later when I was visiting the churches observing the classes as the teachers taught, I remarked that the young lady was not teaching. I learned from the pastor that she was pregnant without being married and was under church discipline.

The fourth discipline; we need to join the local church and participate in all the church wide activities. Hebrews 10:19-25, I John 1:7, Psalm 119:63 are the principal references for this discipline.

What is the explanation of the I AM Bible study method? It is the personal study of a passage or theme essential for the serious disciple of Christ. The I AM Bible study method is simple, practical and ideal for devotions. This method also lends itself to writing Sunday school lessons. I credit the discipline of this method and especially the application for enabling me to write eight years of Sunday school lessons. This method consists of three parts: Investigation or researching of a passage or subject, Application of the truth or truths, and Memorization of the passage for power in living the spiritual life!

There are two types of studies. You can study a subject such as prayer but possessing a STRONG's concordance is essential. You can also study a passage of Scripture. For example, every year I study Psalm 119 for several weeks because it is the thermometer of my spiritual life. Ideally, the Bibles every teacher who speaks and understands English should possess are the Life Application Bible and Reese's Chronological Bible. Secondarily I would have a Scofield, Thompson or Open Bible.

Now for the explanation of each part: INVESTIGATION: it is necessary to read AT LEAST twice the passage to be studied. While reading, it is necessary to search for the given theme of the passage. Write briefly in your own words what the passage states. If the text studied is a story; it's important to briefly write the story mentioning all the characters and what they did in the passage. Do not write too much.

In the APPLICATION you need to start with the words "Today or Now Lord I will (or choose)…" Why? Because yesterday is already past, tomorrow is in the future, I need the Bible now or today. I use the word LORD because Jesus is in control and He is my BOSS. He is the Master of my life and should be everyone's! Finally, I use the words I WILL because this is a personal action of my will. I cannot decide for anyone else.

In the MEMORIZATION you decide how important this part becomes. It is necessary to memorize the BIBLE passage that illustrates your application. Whether you memorize the entire verse or only a part, depends on you. I always memorized the part that gave me power to live the victorious Christian life!

Here is an example of this method that is an example of a Bible text. The verse is Psalm 34:1, "I will bless the LORD at all times: His praise shall continually be in my mouth." Read it twice. For the INVESTIGATION: I worship continually the LORD GOD, with my mouth I will praise Him. APPLICATION; Today, Lord I will worship YOU by praising your name in song. MEMORIZATION: Psalm 34:1, "I will bless the LORD at all times."

Next is an example of a Subject: PEACE. This is a study on only a few of the verses listed in Strong's concordance. I strongly urge those who study a subject to search out and study all the references on a specific subject. In this example we only studied a few. They are: Isaiah 26:3, "Thou wilt keep him in perfect peace, whose mind is stayed on thee: because he trusted in thee." Philippians 4:6-7, "Be careful for nothing; but in everything by prayer and supplication with thanksgiving let your requests be made known unto God. And the peace of God which passeth all understanding, shall keep your hearts and minds through Christ Jesus." John 14:27, "Peace I leave with you, my peace I give unto you; not as the world giveth, give I unto you. Let not your heart be troubled, neither let it be afraid." Remember it is important to read the passages at least twice!

INVESTIGATION: God reserves a perfect peace when I place my confidence in Him. This peace is in Christ Jesus. This peace is for those who place their entire life in Christ.

APPLICATION: Today Lord I will by faith place all my problems in you and ask for your peace.

MEMORIZATION: John 14:27, "Peace I leave with you, my peace I give unto you.

Now I will give you an example of how to do a story using the I AM Bible study method. Remember to read it at least twice. The text is Matthew 18:1-6, "at the same time came the disciples unto Jesus, saying, who is the greatest in the kingdom of heaven? And Jesus called a little child unto him, and set him in the midst of them, and said, Verily I say unto you, except ye be converted, and become as little children, ye shall not enter into the kingdom of heaven. Whosoever therefore shall humble himself as this little child, the same is greatest in the kingdom of heaven. Whoso shall receive one such little child in my name receiveth me. But whoso shall offend one of these little ones which believe in me, it were better for him that a millstone were hanged about his neck, and that he were drowned in the depth of the sea."

The theme of this passage is humility is the secret.

INVESTIGATION: The disciples of Jesus were together and discussing who was the most important. Jesus came bringing a small child and placed him in their midst and told them to repent of their arrogance and spoke of the danger of offending a child.

APPLICATION: Today Lord I repent of my arrogance and ask you to help me think humbly.

MEMORIZATION: Matthew 18:4, "Whosoever therefore shall humble himself as this little child, the same is greatest in the kingdom of heaven."

The next or sixth course we taught was Sunday School Administration. From the beginning, this course was controversial because people tend to have strong opinions about the necessity of recording church attendance and offerings. One missionary went so far as to warn that registering the newly saved was risky.

I will always be thankful to Israel Nadebai, the Seymour hospital administrator who supported and helped me with this course. Among other things, he taught me the proper terms for the attendance books. He also supplied materials such as the grass for the thatch buildings that housed the Sunday school classes at Koumra. His wife Leah was one of our original Sunday school teachers and was still teaching when I left Chad. Thank you Leah!

What is a good definition of Sunday school administration? Sunday school administration is the action of administrating not only the finances and materials, but more importantly, organizing the people in each class. The Bible is full of examples as to the importance of organization and order (I Corinthians 14:40;16:1;Colossians 2:5; Genesis 15:2; 43:16; and Titus 1:7 are only a few). Genesis 15:2 speaks of a steward, and in Genesis 43:16 it says that Joseph was employed as a ruler of the house. In this course the basics of successful administration are explained.

A major part of Sunday school administration dealt with properly recorded reports and attendance records. In many third world countries, such as Chad, church attendance is never printed in the church bulletin but is read verbally at the end of the morning service. Usually, Sunday school starts around 7:30 A.M. and goes for about one hour. This allows the girls time to return to their homes in order to babysit their baby brothers or sisters while their mothers attend the morning service. In all my years in Chad I never encountered a building or room designated the church nursery. Typically, the morning worship service starts around 9:00 or 9:30A.M. and finishes by noon.

The daily report is given verbally by the church secretary at the end of the morning worship service. Included in this report are the following: the total number of attendees usually put into the following categories: boys, girls, and then the total. Secondly, the names of those who made salvation decisions that day with their ages and names of their parents; the names of those who made other decisions; and finally the offering. Sometimes there is also a distinction made between boys' and girls' offerings, but I find it better to just give the total amount. In Chad, it was normal for the girls' offerings to be more than the boys'!

The next report was the monthly or trimester report. Each church should decide how often they want to give this report. Again, I want to mention the fact that in Chad having detailed written records was NOT the norm. I was always astonished at how much the people remembered of the verbal reports. During the first year I was in Koumra, we compiled monthly records and discussed them with the pastor and the deacons. This is NOT common. In fact, many pastors never even ask for the detailed reports! Included in the detailed reports are the following: the total number of students who attended that month. The total number of salvation decisions for that month. The total number of other decisions, if known. I will always remember the children who came to the teacher and asked him to pray for them because they were always quarreling and getting into fights. They knew it was sin but they still wanted to fight and even bite!

The total number of visits made to children in the class. Teachers are expected to visit the homes of the children who have made any decision within the first two weeks of that decision. Also, each child in the class should be visited at their home at least once if not twice a year. The total number of outings with the children and any pertinent details. The total number of children baptized. At first, we did not see many children getting baptized in Chad. However, as time went on, as many as eleven or twelve children especially from the Sarh, Koumra, and Donio areas were baptized. In May 2011, eleven children from

Donio were baptized; and when I left Chad, there were four children in my Sunday school class at Balimba preparing to be baptized! A year later when I visited, all four had been baptized and at least two were planning to be Sunday school teachers when they turned 16!

Also included in this report were the total number of children's deaths. In the past year in the Sarh area alone, several children had died from either drowning, falling from trees during the harvest of mangoes (generally March through May), or from malaria. One child fell out of a mango tree and broke his neck. Attending the funeral for one of these children is always heartrending. However, it can spawn a revival among the children. I remember how one class of 3rd and 4th graders grew from 16 to over 30 after the death of a child because the children in the class were determined to bring their friends to church so that they could get saved.

Also reported in this report is the total amount of the Sunday school offering. Many churches allow the Sunday school superintendent to keep the offerings separate but require the director or treasurer to keep records of expenses for materials bought. For instance, the superintendent would purchase the Sunday school materials, record keeping books, chalk for blackboards, etc. Sometimes even rugs for the smaller children to sit on were purchased with the offerings. The normal classrooms had a dirt floor and the rugs helped protect the children's clothing.

The total amount of tithe given in Sunday school. This did not happen often, but occasionally a Sunday school class needed money for a special project. If the church did not have the finances, then the class would need to raise the funds. Usually the classes raised a crop such as peanuts or cotton or made something and then sold it. They used the money earned to fund the special project. They also tithed 10% of the earnings to the church.

The total amount of gifts given. Any type of gift that is given is recorded in this report. Several times one of our ladies' groups gave a small children's class a big heavy plastic floor covering because the children would fall off the benches. Another time, fathers in Balimba gave roofing material (thatch) for a new classroom. Another example was a deacon who sent strong "shi" (very sugary tea) to the teen age boys who were making mud bricks for a first and second grade classroom.

Also mentioned in this monthly report was the total amount of expenses entailed. We kept our books from January to December. The prayer requests were noted. Often the prayer requests were for ill parents and unsaved family members. Building projects or teaching seminars were noted. We kept a record of not only current projects but also seminars that the teachers were interested in attending. Finally, the names of the Sunday school teachers and the members of each class were noted in the report.

The annual report is the total of all the monthly reports. In Chad, the churches met in Sarh for the annual association meeting during the second half of January. This meeting usually lasted 4 days. Each region (there were 9) presented their annual report at this time.

To make these reports the following necessary account books were needed to make factual reports. Each class needs to be held accountable and kept honest by recording important information and details in account books. Our Sunday school superintendent or secretary kept our books. Each church decided for itself how they wanted to organize it.

The account book of names is the first book. Each class should have their own book. The teacher marks the date, boys present, girls present, amount of the offering, decisions made with their parents' names, and the teacher's name. We had a simple 32 page tablet that cost about $.75 and used about half a page each Sunday. At the end of the year, these tablets were placed in the church archives.

Another account book was the account book of offerings and expenses. It is important to keep this book in perfect order. In my experience, most Sunday school superintendents maintain these books carefully, although there are exceptions. Even gifts such as tea or wood or other items should be recorded. The following categories need to be included: date, designation, receipt, disbursement, total amount remaining, and signatures.

The account book of visits is also necessary. Every visit made by a teacher or Sunday school superintendent should be marked in this book which the secretary or superintendent maintains. The date, name of children visited, pertinent details such as parents present, address of child, etc. should be recorded. I normally mentioned if a family had younger children or visiting children in this report. I endeavored to record the pertinent details within 24 hours of the visit.

The next account book recorded special meetings of teachers' meetings. Each report should include the date of the meeting, names of the participants, where the meeting took place, and any subjects that were discussed or decisions that were made. For example, our teachers met with the Sunday school superintendent in September to discuss that year's Christmas program.

The last book was the attendance book. The name of each child who attends more than 3 times is recorded in this book. The date of the attendance is marked or the reason of the absence if known. The names of the teachers as well as any visitors are also given. Each notebook needs to be kept current. Our teachers were supposed to fill out the attendance book before they left their classroom at the end of the hour.

The second major part of Sunday school administration concerns the roles.

The first major role is the Sunday school superintendent. In Chad, the superintendent serves as the spokesperson for the teachers in the local church. Normally, the teachers would go first to the superintendent instead of the pastor if there was a concern about their class. The superintendent shouldered the following responsibilities:

> 1. He regularly visited each class and gave a report to the church.2. He checked that the teachers were progressing correctly.

3. He decided the number of children in each class.

4. He knew the parents of each child and checked with them regularly as to the progress of each child.

5. He should be a married man with a solid Bible knowledge of all 66 books of the Bible. He should be able to teach the class in the event a teacher is sick. Ideally, he should be a solid spiritual man that everyone respects.

The next major role is the treasurer. This person is responsible for the Sunday school offerings if these offerings are to be kept separate from the regular church collection. Many of our churches started out keeping the offerings separate, but in the last eight years there has been a trend towards incorporating the Sunday school offerings into the church treasury. Especially in the rural areas, sometimes other things besides money are given. I know of several instances where chickens and peanuts as well as squash were received from children as offerings. In these cases, the treasurer was charged to sell these items and place the money into the offering box!

The next role is that of the secretary. This person is to keep track of all written materials, maintain the different notebooks, and write all correspondence. This role may be incorporated into the church secretary's responsibilities.

The final role to be discussed is the role of the local church. The Sunday school is an integral service of the church. Ideally, there should be classes for everyone not just children. Normally, children as young as three years old are capable of learning about the Bible in particular Jesus Christ. Their attention span is short but they can memorize Scripture, start learning songs as well as short stories if accompanied with pictures. Children are the church of the future! Matthew 28:19-20.

The local church needs to be aware of what is being taught to their children. Teachers should not be responsible for purchasing the materials for their class. The local church should provide a quiet, calm, but challenging area to learn.

The church should regard their Sunday school teachers as co-workers of the pastor (Ephesians 4:11; I Corinthians 12:28). It is very important to carefully choose Sunday school teachers!

The church needs to allow the teacher enough time to adequately teach the children. In Chad, the main church auditorium was often used for the classroom of the smaller children. Often people would come in and walk around while the teacher was still teaching and this distracted the children.

Finally the church needs to help the superintendent explain to parents the importance of children consistently attending Sunday school. In Chad I called this problem the "two b's"-babies and beef. Often the mothers would insist that the girls who were 9 or 10 take their baby brothers and sisters ages 15 months to 3 years old) with them to Sunday school. The babies would start crying after 15 minutes and the girls would have to leave and therefore miss half the lesson! The boys, on the other hand, had to take care of the cattle and miss Sunday school entirely even though we were usually finished by 9 A.M.

The next course we taught in training the Sunday school teacher was an abbreviated course on prayer. This course on prayer was first introduced as part of the teacher-training manual when I discovered that most young people being trained, thought prayer meant only asking for things. The first pastor to teach this course in our workshop was Yambaye Ferdinand and the translator of the Sara Madjingaye New Testament. He was killed along with Pastor Ngondedgi Ruben on the way home from Am-Timan when the truck they rode hit a road mine. They had spent their vacation witnessing in an area very resistant to the gospel. Pastor Djimouko Edouard of Banda/Sarh, a dentist, then revised the course and this is the result. Normally the course takes two and a half to three hours, if you look up all the verses. I highly recommend looking up all the references with the students during the course time instead of just verbally reading them. At the end of the workshop, we ask the trainees for their evaluation, and often the students would state that this course had greatly enriched their spiritual lives.

What is your definition of prayer? Here is mine. Prayer is an agreeable communication with and to God. It should be practiced with fervency and in the attitude of submission. Prayer is so powerful because the entire Trinity is involved. I pray to God the Father in the name of the LORD Jesus Christ with the power of the Holy Spirit.

There are many reasons for prayer. I will share with you my key reasons according to the Bible.

1. Luke 22:42-We pray because Jesus Himself prayed.
2. John 15:7-We need to abide in Christ in order to have an effectual prayer life.

3. Matthew 7:7-When we pray, we have the opportunity to see how God will answer our prayers!
4. Revelation 4:11-We can adore or worship God in prayer.
5. Matthew 6:3-6-Prayer allows us to thank God for all His benefits.
6. Psalm 51; I John 1:9-We can confess and repent of our sin in prayer.
7. Colossians 1:9-We can intercede for others in prayer.
8. Matthew 6:7-8-We can ask God to direct us in prayer.
9. Matthew 6:9-10-We can ask for strength and victory over temptation.

Now we are going to examine several good examples of prayer:

1. Luke 18:13-14-Jesus states that this man returned to his home with his sins forgiven because he had prayed in humility with a repentant heart.
2. I Kings 3:9-King Solomon reveals his servant's attitude when he asks God to give him an understanding heart in order to judge God's people.

3. I Kings 8:23-Solomon worships and thanks God in prayer.
4. I Kings 18:36-38-Elijah prays with faith and confidence as does James in James 1:6-8 and likewise Jesus in Mark 11:24.
5. Luke 18:1-5-Jesus tells the parable of the widow as an example of perseverance in prayer.
6. Ephesians 3:16-19- We are enjoined to pray as Paul did in an attitude of love and with intelligence for our friends.
7. Summary: We should pray intelligently with confidence to God; with a contrite, humble, and repentant heart desire to give all the glory to Him; and with faith, love, and perseverance expect to receive an answer.

Now we are going to examine several bad examples of prayer:

1. Luke 18:10-12 reveals a man full of arrogance and self-righteousness. God knows the heart and thoughts of each person (Proverbs 15:29).
2. John 9:31; Isaiah 1:15; and Psalm 66:18 show God's attitude about a sinful heart and what the condition of the heart should be.
3. In Matthew 6:5, God instructs us that He abhors the hypocritical attitude of wanting to be seen praying publically.

4. Matthew 6:7-8 warns us not to use vain repetitions in our prayers.
5. Acts 12:15 speaks of Christians who prayed but doubted that God would answer their prayers. We are not to doubt the power of God!
6. Summary: We should not pray if our heart is arrogant, if we desire admiration for our manner of praying, if we repeat vain repetitions, or speak without reflecting on what we say. Also, we should not pray if we guard sin in our heart or believe that God does not answer prayer.

How are we to pray?

1. We can pray anywhere in any position. Jesus prayed standing upright (Luke 3:21), on his knees (Luke 22:41), and in a special place (Luke 11:1).
2. Daniel prayed three times daily (Daniel 6:10); I Thessalonians 5:17 tells us to "pray without ceasing."
3. The Bible teaches that we can pray with many Christians (Acts 12:12) or alone.

One of the most important prayers for our children to learn is the prayer prayed by Jesus when His disciples asked Him to teach them to pray. Matthew 6:9-13; Luke 11:2-4 is vitally important for the

Christian's daily prayer. We study and memorize this prayer with the 5-7 year olds, with the hope that they will pray openly. If we sense that it is becoming just vain repetition, we stop for awhile. Our goal with the smaller children is to have them memorize this prayer in order to learn to pray voluntarily.

OUR FATHER: God the Father has first place; Christians can pray directly to Him.

WHICH ART IN HEAVEN: God is in heaven preparing a place for us.

HALLOWED BE THY NAME: We honor and respect Him because He is holy.

THY KINGDOM COME: God is king, and Jesus will reign here on earth one day!

THY WILL BE DONE: We desire God's will not our own to be done.

IN EARTH, AS IT IS IN HEAVEN: On earth as well as in heaven where the angels obey.

GIVE US THIS DAY OUR DAILY BREAD: We ask God to provide our daily needs.

AND FORGIVE US OUR DEBTS, AS WE FORGIVE OUR DEBTORS: As we forgive others, God pardons us.

AND LEAD US NOT INTO TEMPTATION: We ask God to help us not to give into temptation.

BUT DELIVER US FROM EVIL: Satan is the greatest enemy of God as well as all Christians.

FOR THINE IS THE KINGDOM, AND THE POWER, AND THE GLORY FOR EVER: After we ask Him for our daily needs, we need to thank him and remember his greatness as the eternal King.

AMEN: This is the Hebrew word meaning, "Think on this truth!" What a great prayer! It can also be used to teach children how to pray on their own.

We finish this abbreviated course on prayer by looking at several other great prayers that are found in the Bible! By no means is this an exhaustive study! John 17:1-26 where Jesus is praying as high priest. IN verses 1-19, Jesus is praying for His disciples. In verses 20-26, Jesus is praying for those who will be saved!

In Colossians 1:9-11 and Philippians 1:8-11, we are challenged to intercede for other Christians.

In I Timothy 2:1-4, we are charged to pray for the whole world as well as those in authority.

In Matthew 5:44, we Christians are told to pray for our enemies! In Matthew 9:38, Jesus Christ charges us to pray that God would send forth workers for His field.

In Mark 14:38, Jesus is in the garden praying and finds Simon sleeping. He charges the disciples to watch and pray that they do not fall into temptation. James 5:13 tells us we are to pray for the afflicted and ill!

It needs to be mentioned that until the capability of cell phones arrived in Chad we also taught a course on letter writing. The French system of letter writing is different from ours. The reason the course of letter writing was introduced was due to the fact that one time I received a hand written letter. It was written to me with a date that showed it took at least a month to find me though it was written in Chad. There was no sending address or name written. The letter explained a major problem but I had no means of responding! It was only later when Pastor Machine, the driver, and I were visiting with the churches that had a Sunday school in the Koumra area that we discovered the author of the letter! When the teacher asked me why I had not responded to the letter I brought out the letter and asked him why he had not stated who had sent it!

The final course we taught in the workshops is somewhat of a review as well as introducing some teaching methods. Teaching methods or pedagogy permits the teacher to clearly and engagingly teach. This is basic and essential to education. This is why it is very important to know how to teach and to understand the principles of teaching. We desire to see fruit produced by our students.

What is pedagogy (teaching methods)? Pedagogy is an art, the science of teaching. It is a series of laws, or consecutive principles where the goal is receiving an education. In Sunday school, our goal is that the children will clearly learn principally about Jesus Christ being Savior since He was born to die on the cross so that we can have eternal life. We also want our children to learn about the people of the Bible and clearly explain their contribution to us.

What is education? It is the training and development of the intelligence of the individual. The word education is reserved for humans. Education can be both formal and informal. Sunday school is formal religious training whereas working with a child in the garden and explaining how God created the world is informal learning. Every society has a form of both formal and informal learning.

What are the goals of religious education? In reviewing education and in particular Sunday school goals Matthew 28:19-20 clearly states our goal of reaching the nations. Children are part of the nations, and teaching them. We are to bring them to Christ and then help them become disciples. Briefly: 1. Present opportunities to believe and confess Jesus Christ as their Savior. 2. Present occasions to obey God starting with baptism. 3. Present times for them to serve God.

What are the resources or manner of education? There are both means and procedures in education and here are some of them: The methods, systems or means to a goal. The first to know is the method of statement or exposition: in this method, the teacher speaks only without discussion of those listening. No one is permitted to ask questions until the end. This method allows the teacher to win time to present information but this is not a good method for teachers who work with the children under 10 years of age.

The next method or system involves questioning the students. This method involves asking many questions of the students by the teacher with the goal in mind that the students will discover the answers. This process prods the students to search for answers and arrive at the answers themselves. This method is not good for the under 10 years of age group.

The mixed method or system is the next method. This method is a mixture of the exposition and questioning methods. This method is very active and is the best method for children of ages 5 and older. In this method the teacher helps the student find the answers by asking questions which help the child find the answer.

The dogmatic method is where the teacher obliges the students to memorize the material. Regarding the Sunday school class, this is the method the teacher uses when causing the students to memorize Bible verses. In the older child, when he is learning the names of the books of the Bible, this method is being utilized. If a child has been with you at least one year and is entering 4th grade, he should know the books of the Bible and be proficient in Sword Drills. In a sword drill the leader instructs all the participants to have their Bibles flat on the table or in their laps, closed. Then the leader quotes twice the reference and says go. The first person to find the reference stands and reads the verse. Finally, for the child six and below the dogmatic method is the best method.

Briefly, in teaching effectively, the teacher should be capable of employing all these methods and should use a variety of these methods when teaching. The best methods for children under the age of 12 are a combination of the mixed and dogmatic methods.

What are the procedures of education: like methods, the procedures of teaching employed by Sunday school teachers are several: Here are the most common and effective:

1. The procedure of explanation: this procedure consists of usage of a blackboard or visual object. Students retain easily what they see! This procedure is excellent for children ages 3 through 12!
2. The experimentation procedure: in this procedure, testing the child by giving questions or an essay is implemented. In Chad at the end of each lesson book, the teacher gave a test whereby he asked questions and also required to recite memory verses by giving the reference and the child quoting the verse. We found that children over 8 years of age could quote more than 25 verses in this manner!
3. The application procedure: the teacher knew the child had learned correctly when he witnessed the change in the student's life. Often when the story of Cain and Abel was taught in Chad and how Abel died we would witness how this story caused the boys especially ages 7 and older remark they would never fight again.

4. The procedure of testing: here testing by questions and recitations are employed. Especially at Christmas and sometimes Easter when the children participated in the Christmas program reciting Luke 2, this procedure reveals whether the student truly understood the importance of Christ's birth!

Briefly: the participation of the children in the classroom is absolutely necessary! A person retains only 10% of what he hears, 70% of what he sees, and 90% of what he does! Knowing and utilizing a variety of methods and procedures is essential for the teacher when teaching!

Now we will study the teacher or educator! The teacher is someone who trains others. The job of teaching is delicate. Consequently, the teacher needs to prepare carefully. The preparation of the teacher is the secret of successful teaching. Teaching is a difficult art and demands much preparation. To achieve success in this noble task the educator needs the following qualifications physically, intellectually, morally and socially:

1. Physically, he should enjoy good health as preparations requires physical preparations. The teacher should employ a clear, pleasant but

distinct voice. His manner of dressing should be dignified not provacative. It should be such that it attracts the students to listen to what he is saying. He should be modest and clean!
2. Intellectually, he should be able to carry on a good conversation with the students. He should be able to engage in conversation in a pleasant manner yet exciting them to think more profoundly.
3. Morally he should be:
   a. Punctual: he should arrive at least 15 minutes before the children arrive for the purpose of readying his class room.
   b. Patient: he should be patient for the purpose of supporting the weaknesses of the others in the class without getting angry.
   c. Joyful: the teacher needs to be welcoming with a smile on his or her face always desiring to be welcoming. In this way, the students are attracted to what is being taught.
   d. Just: the teacher needs to always be just in his actions when problems arise and they certainly will when you have a large group of children in your class under 8 years old.
   e. Calm and impartial love: loving your students and letting them know you care

about them by visiting them at their homes several times a year is a powerful way to reach and make a difference.
f. Self-control: a teacher who cannot control especially his tongue causes enormous problems.
g. Model: the teacher must practice what he teaches!

Spiritually the teacher must be a witness to what he teaches. It is essential that he be saved, baptized, and in full communion of his local church!

Now we will be discussing the subjects of discipline and authority in the classroom. The definition of discipline involves following rules and regulations that promote order. This permits order in the classroom and reinforces the authority of the teacher. Keeping order or discipline permits learning to take place which is the goal.

Preparing well the lesson is the secret of success in the classroom. A teacher cannot be too prepared. Joshua 1:1-9, and Matthew 28:18-20.

Review: the teacher who remains calm and in control when faced with difficult situations will be respected. The person who sees each of his students as a creation of God and practices the seven laws of teaching, will succeed.

We cannot end this section labeled 'what' without discussing the important activity of singing in the Sunday school program. I know that Chadian children love to sing. About half of my Sunday school class in Balimba came twice a week to learn the songs they had not learned in the Chantons en Coeur! (Choruses/Songs of the Heart) I also know that the children in Rachel's Sunday school class at Matadi Baptist Church in Monrovia, Liberia as well as some of the children of the Bible school students in Tappita loved to sing.

During the course of the workshop we would endeavor to learn at least 15 songs and choruses. In Chad, thanks to Ruth Bartow and Ada Temple who compiled the Chantons en Coeur (Songs of the Heart) there were over one hundred twenty songs. I will always praise God for Ruth and Ada who brought them to my attention. In Sunday school we sing choruses more so than hymns as choruses concentrated on one theme and were shorter. When I taught in Liberia we learned and sung about fifteen choruses. They were JOY, This Little Light of Mine, The Wise Man Built, I Have Decided to Follow Jesus, The Alphabet Song, etc.! Many of these songs are action songs. It is vitally important to sing doctrinally sound choruses! Many modern Sunday school songs always speak about 'Me' and not Jesus. Every teacher should know at least 40 choruses.

When?

This part of my book is unusual. Why? Because it is so diverse. I start simply but it develops into something complex. Never did I give birth to physical children, but I was the "spiritual mother" to many. Because I never married, I was physically freer to get involved with activities with nationals. In the course of my thirty-one years of serving in Chad, I spoke with thousands of children in Sunday school class settings, when I visited their church. Many of these children over the age of nine wanted an entire Bible as they would say "You can't read the stories of David and Goliath in the New Testament!" I would tell the children, especially those who had Christian parents, to ask their parents to read a Bible story to them every night. The child was encouraged to listen carefully for the 1) Who are the people mentioned in the passage? 2) What happened in the story? 3) When did this take place? 4) Where did it happen? And, finally, 5) Why did this action take place?

It is amazing how this simple instruction was adopted by the children of Chad because they were hungry to learn and it helped the child comprehend and do better in their schooling! Parents started family devotions and they had better interaction with their kids! I remember one family especially, Marcel and Elisabeth Djimasra. He was the medical evangelist at Balimba for several years and his wife is a Sunday school teacher now in Goro, close to the Chad/Central African Republic border. I first grew to love this family when they lived and worked in the Danamadji area. Gedeon was the baby when I worked with them. I credit Marcel and Elisabeth and their devotion to raising their twelve children including two special needs children: Gedeon and Marjorie (named after me). Gedeon died of cerebral malaria when 17 years of age. Gedeon and Marjorie made professions of faith in Jesus when they were thirteen and eleven while hearing the Easter story. Marcel and Elisabeth, except for Sundays, always have family devotions in the evening. All their children have made professions of faith and several are Sunday school teachers!

Because of Marcel and Elisabeth, I learned that usually children with Down's syndrome, like Gedeon and Marjorie, while still under the age of two were taken by family members (uncles and aunts) into the wilderness or thrown into a river to join their snake family! Yes! You read me correctly! I was astounded when told that even pastor's wives who had been trained biblically believed that Down syndrome children were half human and half snake!

Psalm 119:73, 'Thy hands have made me and fashioned me: give me understanding, that I may learn thy commandments." Quite often, especially while working with my Friday evening 'English conversation classes, I would open up the discussion saying we could discuss any subject they desired. I found that many Chadian Christian young people could not understand why an American woman would allow that person who was developing inside her to be killed. In other words planned abortion. In my thirty one years in Chad I had very few visitors from America because of the enormous expense. But the few who did come, sometimes commented they would often see children as well as adults relieve themselves in plain sight. They sometimes remarked that this was not a very civilized thing to do. I replied that I agreed. But then I told them that Chad had a law that stated if a pregnant woman was hurt intentionally and the woman lived but the baby died, the person who hurt her could be tried for murder. I know of at least one case in the Sarh area where this happened! Chadians know that the little person inside the mother is a human being! Each child is a special creation of God! Children are each nation's greatest treasure!

Another pivotal 'when' in my life that shaped my future ministry was joining Baptist Mid-Missions. I knew that joining an agency/board was essential and I wanted to have the word 'Baptist' in its name because I am a Christian first and an independent Baptist second. People have asked why I had to join an agency and not just let the supporting churches send me monthly checks which I could cash in the country! Since I had forty-two supporting churches and seven individuals in the beginning, this meant I would have to travel to N'djamena to cash the checks. That is easily four days of traveling more likely a week! Suffice it to say that when I first arrived in Chad in December of 1981, personal checks could not be cashed. We would have had to send them back to the mission agency which in turn would make the transaction, sending a legal receipt to the giver and send one bank transfer a month. A mission agency is essential, especially in third world countries like Chad and especially countries where English is not the national language. There are countless reasons why I joined Baptist Mid-Missions but I will elaborate on a few.

I know many missionaries in Africa. Most of them serve in countries where an ocean is part of the border. Baptist Mid-Missions first worked in the interior of Africa. The Republic of Chad formerly was part of French Equatorial Africa. It is surrounded by the following countries going clockwise: Libya, Sudan, Central African Republic, Cameroon and Nigeria. These countries share a continent, not a united nation. There is no Nation of Africa! When you travel from one country to another in Africa you must get a visa to enter! Americans who have never traveled outside of the USA find this hard to understand. Also, in Chad, your organization must be registered with the government. An independent missionary cannot use his or her sending church as her organization.

To work in Chad, you must first be able to communicate in the French language. American checks are in English and therefore many would not be able to understand what is written! Arranging for learning the French language is not something a sending church is equipped to arrange.

Another reason I went with Baptist Mid-Missions is their experience of working in land-locked countries like Chad. There are no railroads in Chad. When you fly to Chad you must land in the capital, N'djamena. They also have the field council principal in place to advise the missionaries. When I arrived in Chad, Dr. David Seymour was the president of the field council of our missionaries. The missionaries at that time were Dr. Dave and Ruth Seymour, Veronica Sisson, Drs. Ron and Martha Snearly, Ruth Bartow, Ada

Temple, and James and Carol King and their three children. I shared with them my testimony and Dr. Dave told me that in this first year in Chad I needed to visit all the mission stations where BMM missionaries lived! This I did! I was also encouraged to learn a tonal language such as Sara Madjingaye. The only way I can learn another language is if I do nothing but study. The one time I was able to leave my other duties and devote myself to learning that language, civil war broke out and we had to leave the country. Because I was part of Baptist Mid-Missions I was able to have an American Express card in case of needing to purchase emergency tickets to leave a country as I never had enough cash on hand to purchase tickets to the states.

Another reason Baptist Mid-Missions and I became partners is financially they handle all the gifts of support. When I first went to Chad in 1981 it took four weeks for a letter from the states at least to get from the States to us in southern Chad. While I was in Koumra, sometimes the cotton company brought the mail to us! The Chadians knew that when the airplane arrived no one should visit the missionaries in the afternoon until they came outside! Why? We were feverishly reading our letters and writing responses as the plane would be leaving the next morning usually for N'djamena! I keenly remember how I gave priority to letters written by children! I always shared in my reply the importance of how long it takes for letters to arrive from the States and vice versa!

This all changed when email, then cell phones, became possible. The first time I had to leave Chad was in September of 1982. No missionary had a land line and email was unknown. We did have radios on each station where you could send short messages but you needed to know the Alpha-Bravo-Charlie-Delta code. "Death squads" because of the government upset were in place and the national Christians wanted us to leave as they were scared for our lives. Rather than going north to N'djamena, Ruth Seymour, Ron and Martha Seymour and I left in the evening with Israel Nadabe driving. Veronica was on the way having been traveling in the Sarh/Danamadji area and Dr. Dave Seymour stayed behind at Koumra. Israel accompanied us to the border at Gore then Ron drove the truck navigating some incredibly bad roads until we arrived in Boguila, Central African Republic. There we stayed until Veronica Sisson joined us and the BMM airplane came from Bangui. It had been about four or five days since we left Koumra. The Snearly's stayed in Boguila as skilled physicians were always welcome, hoping they could return to Chad as they had barely been back from furlough. We three:

Ruth Seymour, Ronnie Sisson and I arrived in Bangui thanks to the BMM pilot. I don't remember much about the long ride by commercial airline until we were flying over the Statue of Liberty in the New York City harbor. I started crying on seeing that lady. By the time we landed, the tears had abated. As the customs official looked through my passport he smiled and said 'welcome home'. Again I cried profusely. He then told me that people were looking for me and that I should call the Baptist Mid-Missions home office. He accompanied me to a private office where I called Cleveland asking for the Africa field administrator, Dr. Buck. No one in the home office had heard from us since we left Koumra! Dr. Buck asked me about everyone and I told him that except for Dr. Dave everyone was coming back to the States and the others should be arriving sometime that day! I was able to call my parents as well as my home church. I flew first to my parents' home in northern Minnesota. Much of my family was waiting for me at the Bemidji airport! Two weeks later I flew to Georgia where I busied myself in raising more support and sharing with people how our omnipotent God works! The point is, that because of the Baptist Mid-Mission agency, funds were advanced so that tickets could be bought to get us out of perilous situations. The Baptist Mid-Missions home office is equipped to handle international emergency conditions!

The Baptist Mid-Missons family exists to strategically advance the building of Christ's church, with His passion and for His glory, in vital partnership with Baptist churches worldwide.

Another major reason I appreciate Baptist Mid-Missions has to do with the field council policy. When I arrived in Chad in December of 1981 it was the first time I set foot in Africa. The field council was there to help me, not smother me! Because of field councils, complex ministries such as the medical as well as the translation ministries prosper and produce fruit. Proverbs 11:14, "Where no counsel is, the people fall: but in the multitude of counsellors there is safety." I remember distinctly when Dr. Dave convened a meeting of the missionaries to discuss the need of translating the complete Bible. We rejoiced when Bibles International, a department of Baptist Mid-Missions, came at the invitation of the field council to oversee the work of translation of the entire Bible not just the New Testament. We knew this was of vital importance! Field councils provide a forum to discuss issues as well as help the missionaries pray more effectively for the various ministries. How happy I will be when the complete

Bibles in the Sara Madjingaye, DAY, NDEM, Sara Kaba Naa, Ngam will be finished!

Baptist Mid-Missions (www.bmm.org) has the foresight to plan for the retirement needs of their missionaries. At this time I live at Missionary Acres in the foothills of the Ozarks. Missouri is a beautiful state in the center of the USA. More states surround Missouri than any other. Starting to the north and going clockwise there is Iowa, Illinois, Kentucky, Tennessee, Arkansas, Oklahoma, Kansas and finally a bit of Nebraska! The scenery here in the foothills is incredible. I can see our fishing pond from my big window! Our homes are well built! I live in a ranch style home that has an attached garage! The views from my office as well as the living room and kitchen are gorgeous! Here in southeast Missouri we enjoy the four seasons. In the springtime you see the redbuds and dogwoods trees amongst the variety of green leaves. I have counted at least 10 different shades of green in early spring! October is also a beautiful time with the oaks, and maples turning their beautiful colors. We are a community of missionaries, retired pastors and not yet retired missionaries who enjoy getting together occasionally to pray as well as socialize and discuss every imaginable topic. You will not find a more patriotic group except for the military. Why? Because many of us have worked in countries where liberty comes at a recognizable price. There are people living here who were in Israel at the time of the war for Israel! I was in Chad and asked to be a witness for the very first presidential election. Never will I forget that Sunday in April when we celebrated Sunday school and church early so that the citizens could go and vote for their president. I witnessed these people stand in the hot (over 100 degrees Fahrenheit) sun for 2 hours before they voted! Later, we learned that 98% of all registered voters in the Sarh area voted in the elections! There is a group of us who meet every Thursday evening to pray for our nation and its leaders! Check us out at

www.missionaryacres.com!

Where?

Chad, Africa first caught my attention while a student at St. Cloud State College (now a university). As one of my electives, I chose a geography course studying Africa. At the time of the course, Chad was embroiled in civil war. I remember thinking that here was a large country approximately two and a half times the state of California in the middle of Africa that had one international airport in the capital, N'djamena and no railroads. Yet the country had unexploited mineral reserves and the lower half had great soil. The population was under five million people because of disease, war, and poverty. It was the poorest country in Africa. It had been part of French Equatorial Africa but gained its independence in 1960. Civil War had broken out. There was no jungle but the savannah climate in the south promoted good crops if the rainy season was adequate. The people were tall because of good protein in the form of peanuts and fish. I remember thinking, "Does God truly care equally for all people?"

I remember arriving in N'djamena in mid-December of 1981 and staying with Miss Dannie Gounoh, a missionary with TEAM(the Evangelical Alliance Mission) for a few days as I had to register with the government and figure out how to get down to Koumra as the MAF plane (Missionary Aviation Fellowship) radio was experiencing radio problems. I will always be indebted to Dannie, Carl Hodges(-TEAM) and Maurice Houriet (MAF) pilot. We were scheduled to leave in pickup trucks as we wanted to celebrate Christmas at Koumra when Maurice came tearing back to the station (5 minutes drive from airport) and said to quickly come as he had just received permission to fly and to hurry up before the air controllers changed their minds!

What an adventure! I love flying in small planes and here I was viewing Chad for about two and a half hours from a five seat Cessna! The ground was basically brown and beige as it was the dry season except for the Chari River which was more gray/beige than blue. I was allowed to ride in the co-pilot seat because this was my first time in Chad! We first flew to Babelim then the next day to Koumra. I will always be indebted to MAF for their service. Finally I was where God had called me and I met my new collegues. Dr. Dave and Ruth had a room for me at their home where I recovered from jet lag. A short time later I experienced my first Chadian Christmas! We spent Christmas morning in our church! It was amazing how these groups of people had memorized their parts which were Bible verses mostly of Luke 2:1-20.

Then they sang Christmas songs that had many verses. I grew tired because many of the recitations were in the Sara Madjingaye language and I did not understand. Truly Christmas was a celebration of the birth of Jesus Christ!

Where were the Sunday school classes? When I first arrived in Koumra, I learned from Dr. Dave and Ruth that every Sunday morning about 7:30 A.M., the children ages three through fourteen met under the metal roof near the hospital and the students of either the Bible School or the medical evangelists in training took turns preaching to these children. I remarked that I would love to observe this class and everyone was glad to know I would be there the next Sunday. I arrived about fifteen minutes before it was supposed to start and already there were about one hundred children present. Pastor M'solnan brought over a young man and said that he would be my translator since I did not speak Sara Madjingaye! To say I was surprised was an understatement! I remember thinking "What am I going to do as I don't have any visuals and LORD You really need to help me!" I had about twenty minutes of preparation time and the story I told is from John 6 about the lad who gave his lunch to Jesus and the five thousand men plus all those children and women were fed. I remember telling the children that you did not have to be a big person to be used of God. I briefly mentioned that the most important decision any person can make was to confess his sin and believe in Jesus Christ to save him because of Jesus shed blood. I then said as I closed that if anyone wanted to talk with us we would be available after wards. Either six or seven boys stayed back and confessed Christ as their Savior! Of those six children, four, when they grew up, became Sunday school teachers and later at least two became pastors!

Why is it Important to Know the Proper Order and Names of the Books in the Bible?

When I was a first grade school teacher I made it a priority to memorize the names of my students the very first day. I wanted them to know that I valued them immediately so that they knew I cared for them and would do everything I could to help them succeed in my classroom.

As an adult, when I attend a church service and it is time for the preaching of the Bible, I delight in searching out the references that the preacher gives us. I am blessed because our pastor would use at least fifteen different references in each sermon, especially in the Sunday evening service. I am also a note taker of the sermons I hear. I always write down the reference as well as find the reference in my Bible. In the church I now attend my ministry revolves around elementary age children. The majority of the children are "bus children" because their parents are not saved. Consequently, these children attend public schools and do not benefit from a home where they are encouraged by parents in biblical studies. The only Bible instruction they receive is at our church. If you do not know the books of the Bible you cannot find them in your Bible. In a good Sunday school by the end of second grade, every child should be able to find all references in the New Testament and by the middle of fourth grade a child should be able to quote all the books of the Bible without having to go to the table of contents to find its page number. 2 Timothy 2:15, "Study to shew thyself approved unto God, a workman that needeth not to be ashamed, rightly dividing the word of truth."

Why is it Important to Have a Separate Bible and Not Just Depend on Your IPAD?

Don't get me wrong! I find IPAD's incredibly helpful when I am teaching especially, but everyone should have their own separate Bible by the time they are eight years old. My very first Bible was given to me by the church when I turned seven years old. It had a beautiful cover of a Bible scene with Jesus talking to children on one side and on the inside were many beautiful pictures of Bible stories. By the time I was in fifth or sixth grade it was worn out. My parents gave me THE OPEN BIBLE. It was a bit more complex and subsequently helpful in my studies. When I first went to Chad, my chief Bible was a Scofield Bible. For my French Bible I used the Louis Segond translation because the Scofield Bible used that translation. I still have it but my favorite Bible is my LIFE APPLICATION BIBLE, KJV. Every Sunday school teacher should have a LIFE APPLICATION BIBLE. As I mentioned before, my parents expected me to treasure my Bible. I was the one responsible to have it ready for church and to bring it to church every time we went to church. The Bible is unique. An IPAD can and is used for many purposes. We must never forget that the Bible is the most important book in the world. Every problem can be resolved if you properly understand all the

Bible teaches. To live the victorious Christian life God desires for all of us, we must have a thorough understanding of all that it teaches. I John 5:3, "For this is the love of God, that we keep his commandments: and his commandments are not grievous. 4. For whatsoever is born of God overcometh the world: and this is the victory that overcometh the world, even our faith. 5. Who is he tht overcometh the world, but he that believeth that Jesus is the Son of God."

Last picture of all of Marji's brother + sisters with their spouses.

Bob Terry Charlie Russ Greg
LuAnn   Marji
   Andrea Naomi Lorna Jenni Ruth

Greg Andrea Jennifer Lorna Marjorie
LuAnn Naomi
Naomi oldest, LuAnn youngest

Roallate Gedeon in red
Pastor Djmouko Edouard - shortest man standing
All others are Sunday school superintends

Pastor Yamalta in blue

Mom/Dad, Naomi by dad, I'm next to mom, Lorna in middle in front of dad's parents home in Chicago.

First Group of Sunday School teachers of Koumra with Marjorie

MARANIE   MAVIS
JENNIFER
LEANA

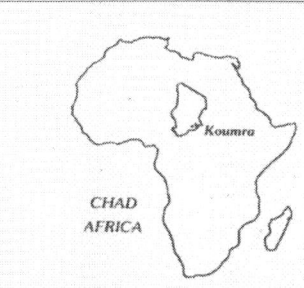

CHAD AFRICA

Field Address:
Le Centre Medical
Baptist Mid-Missions
B.P. 13
KOUMRA, TCHAD
AFRIQUE

Home Address:
R.D. 1, Box 575
New Castle, PA 16105

Home Office:
Baptist Mid-Missions
P.O. Box 308011, Cleveland, Ohio 44130-8011

Dr. Dave and Ruth Seymour

Galatians 6:2: "Bearing one another's burdens."

Helping the local churches in
Medical Evangelism

Pastor Yamalta in blue
my Datsun / Balimba
I don't know man in long gown

Crossing the river in Chad '93 or '94

Susan Hossack

Jakobed wife of → Pastor Takia Missi Antoine

Made in the USA
Lexington, KY
10 September 2018